WASTE OF MONEY

WASTE OF MONEY

Overspending in Football
A Tragic Loss To The Beautiful Game

Paul Stenning

Published By Know the Score Books

A2 Yeoman Gate
Yeoman Way
Durrington
BN13 3QZ

Web: www.knowthescorebooks.com

First published 2010

ISBN: 9781905411931

A catalogue record for this book is available from the British Library.

Typeset in Adobe Caslon Pro 11pt/14pt

Printed and bound in Great Britain by CPI Group

ACKNOWLEDGEMENTS

I would like to thank all who have helped in the creation of this book, many who offered casual tips and suggestions which often led down an interesting new route: to my many private sources who wish to remain confidential; to Nick Szczepanik for editorial assistance and advice. In particular, I express my gratitude to my publishers Know the Score Books for ensuring my original vision received the right type of passion and investment. I would like to dedicate this book to my wonderful wife Isla and beautiful daughter Samantha for all their love and support.

CONTENTS

INTRODUCTION

Today the game of football is in a perilous state and it's all to do with two things: money and greed. Many people who have followed football for more than 15 years will tell you that the game became more about money with the advent of Sky television's takeover of the sport and the introduction of a Premiership in the early 1990s. Though many would also concede that the sport became reinvigorated and more exciting with the focus on better television coverage, we tend to lament the good old days when the game was made up of mostly British players who played for the love of the game as opposed to a fortune in weekly wages, when tackles weren't outlawed for touching bone and when nobody dived. There was certainly no lack of skill to the game of times past, most people consider the likes of Pele and George Best to be amongst the greatest players of all time and both were head and shoulders above most revered players in the modern game.

So, let's get it clear: for the most part we are not simply nostalgic about the game as it used to be, it really was better in many respects. The prevalence of money in the modern era has ruined the spirit of the game, if nothing else. Previously, for the most part, chairmen and owners of clubs were not in it to make a profit or quick turnover – they were in charge of clubs they had a special affinity for and thus this translated to the managers and players being chosen with the same reverence. In turn, the game was played with passion and integrity, instead of for some wider fortune chasing scheme.

What Sky's presence certainly did do is provide a multitude of businessmen with no connection or particular knowledge or experience of football to become involved in lieu of personal gain. The beginning of this was perhaps the introduction of shirt sponsors in the late 1970s – once one company could be seen to make a profit off a football club, it would obviously follow that others would want in on the act as well. Yet where football programmes tended to feature local businesses which would provide for a club's outward community, shirt sponsors often had no relation to the locality of a club – thus, big name overseas products such as Hitachi, Talbot and Saab were amongst the first major shirt sponsors. To begin with, even the likes of ITV and the BBC – then the only channels available in the UK – frowned upon shirt sponsorship, and refused to allow televised matches of teams wearing a company's name across their front. Yet it only took a few years for the potential money making of this idea to gel with the heads of the TV companies and soon both the BBC and ITV were televising teams with companies blazoned across their chests, realising the marketing potential of this was very lucrative.

Perhaps the real genius of this initial plan was when clubs began to sell replica shirts in the late 1980s. Not only could fans wear the shirt of their club, they were advertising too. Fans became walking billboards, carrying the proud crest of their club whilst reminding passers by that Draper Tools was where they should visit for that hammer they'd been after. Though the company logos were often ugly and certainly unconventional to the purpose of a football shirt, to an extent there was an understanding and acceptance that this was just one step ahead from advertising hoardings around the pitch or adverts in the club programme.

Yet the clubs began to exploit the fans' hunger to support the club, first by changing the replica kit every season, and then agreeing to change it only every two years but introducing a third kit which was rarely worn by the team, despite being lapped up by merchandise buyers.

After the Premier League was launched in 1992, the next line of profiteering came in the form of player names on the back of shirts, with fans paying a premium extra for the benefit of the same names as their idols on their overpriced replica kits. The right number, and league patches, were also part of the package. The miracle fabrics that were supposedly part of the shirts – those that claimed to keep the player warm when it was cold and cool when they sweated, by drawing moisture away from the body – were described by one manufacturer in a moment of honesty as being "all polyester and it comes from the same source – it's all crap".

Clubs were reprimanded soon after the Premier League initiative for fixing prices between themselves and manufacturers and particular sportswear retailers, pushing any potential discount retailers out of the market. Yet this trend still continues today, with replica shirts that cost under £5 to make often being sold on for up to £50 or £60 with all the requisite additions. In 2006/07 the next stage in the ludicrous thirst for sponsorship was integrated, with additional advertising now coming on the back of shirts, and in Scotland on shorts as well. Soon, no doubt, a top British player will look more like a Formula One driver than a footballer.

In truth, the advertising on shirts and the monopoly of the main manufacturers such as Nike, Adidas and Puma is the tip of the iceberg. The real inundation of wasteful bundles of money has come in the form of stadium naming rights and the owners of clubs themselves who often have a vast array of different business interests of which football is only a small part. Their modus operandi is often to have fun with a football club, in the same way they might enjoy buying luxury yachts, sports cars and even submarines (ask Roman).

The last few years have seen a quick, overbearing influx of foreign investors and businessmen who are so rich they often reach the heights of the *Forbes* rich list. We have seen a mass of Asian and Middle Eastern investment and with this has come a dominance in the highest areas of footballing investment. It is just the beginning that Arsenal's Highbury ground lost decades of sporting tradition in its name change to the Emirates Stadium. The owners at Manchester City and Portsmouth have signalled a changing of the guard. Money has always talked but it talks loudest when backed up by oil barons and sultans, those with wealth that far exceeds the Premier League itself, never mind the individual teams within it.

Yet given their lack of experience at running a football club, quite often these billionaires are merely playing with the traditions and background of a football club, with apparently little concern for the consequences and people involved in the process of their fumbling. A football club is now seen as a method of profit, a corporation running for the purposes of revenue and little else. The future outcome of this meddling can only be that the middle to smaller clubs will drop in interest to the league itself, unless they are taken over by another billionaire business man or company – such as with Notts County who were recently taken over by Qadbak Investments, a cloak and dagger company who "represent certain Middle Eastern and European based investment families".

The future of the game can really only fall under two possibilities: either the game as we know it will collapse, or the game will ultimately be run by billionaires, oil conglomerates, corporations and banks. We are already halfway there. This would mean in effect that there is next to no chance for fans of a club to have any real power in the running of their life, their passion. Even wealthy fans or associates have been pushed out in recent times by the power of the billionaires. For evidence of this, see the likes of Chris Mort and a consortium of local northeast investors who sought to take over Newcastle United from Mike Ashley and end his fairly dire reign at the helm of the club. They were pushed out of contention by their failure to raise more than £70m of initial investment, despite having the best interests of the club at heart and far more money-making potential for the future because of it – Alan Shearer, the Tyneside legend, would have been installed as manager under Mort, for instance.

Even knowledgeable and experienced football men don't stand a chance in the current day and age. After making a name for himself in Singapore with his work for ESPN, former Everton and Liverpool footballer Steve McMahon joined the Singapore based Profitable Group as their commercial director, and as part of this led a charge to take over Everton. After a rebuff in Merseyside, Profitable were allegedly eager to take over Newcastle, though after a lack of communication from Ashley the deal fell through.

The future appears to be that football will be dominated by global businesses and extremely wealthy individuals, which means more expense for the average fan and a decrease of traditions within the game. Yet it is possible for sports to still be fun as well as profitable. The National Football League (NFL) in America is a very good example of this, where team shirts don't feature adverts and there are no advertising hoardings shadowing the ground. They are not teams really, though, every one of the 32 who make up the league are referred to as franchises. In America there is no pussyfooting around, the fans know they are part of a massive financial conglomerate but they also know that come Sunday it is all about the game. Yet even here, worryingly, the traditional names of the stadiums of old such as Indianapolis Colts' Hoosier Dome have been replaced, first with the RCA Dome and now the Lucas Oil Stadium (a deal which will cost the oil company $120m over a 20-year period) – a worrying shade of things to come.

There was some hope that with Tampa Bay Buccaneers' owners the Glazer family taking over affairs at Manchester United that there might be some upturn and fresh impetus into the way association football is run. Yet their involvement seems again to be more about profiteering than any real passion for the game or desire to improve upon its current state.

This book is about money in football and the most glaring examples of where it has gone, or been wasted. Whilst it would have been perhaps understandable to focus on the ownership struggles at Liverpool, Manchester United and Manchester City, it would also have been predictable. The book aims to uncover the riddles behind many key deals or figureheads in the current game as well as to look at less obvious examples and stories of corporate greed and/or stupidity.

This may be a damning indictment of the current state of the game behind the scenes, and those who control it, but it is also an occasionally amusing look at the vast swathes of money wasted in pursuit of player gold or in some cases, sushi.

The stories within this book may be separate examples, but they are inextricably linked by owners, chairman and investors with very poor money management skills, and ultimately the only ones to suffer from this are football lovers and fans. As well as revealing the most blatant, ridiculous and revealing episodes of money excess, I will also examine what can be done in order to remedy the ongoing problems all football clubs are seemingly bound to face. In 2010 the game rapidly needs a rethink and an overhaul if it is to retain any semblance of the "beautiful" tag it has managed to uphold for many years. If there is no limit to financial excess then there is no limit to the depths those with the money can plunge the game.

WASTE OF MONEY!

AUTHOR'S NOTE

In the mid 1990s I worked for a small financial advisory firm who handled the finances of the pop group Take That as well as a handful of high profile celebrity clients. This was my first taste of how the other side lived. Their incomings were enormous, their personal spending superfluous, and yet their finances were immaculate. Each member of the band – aside from Robbie Williams, who even then was handled by a different company – spent heavily, but they also spent within their means, which was an unwritten rule set by we who handled their money and their bank statements and investments. Here's your spending money, here's what you should save. And they did save. Their investments were exemplary – £10,000 repeated in several portfolios which were safe, £5,000 repeated in those which were less secure. But their money grew and they were extremely well off even when they had called it a day and there was apparently no more musical success around the corner.

Today of course they are a much loved institution and still, no doubt, financially astute. Their return to the music scene was not, as often is the case with so many former pop stars, borne of a need to make money back that they lost in their career first time around, but rather because they *wanted* to get back together – the money made in the process was merely a welcome addition. Finances which are handled well from the beginning are rarely likely to trip you up later down the line.

Towards the end of the 1990s I was part of a company that booked bands for concerts around the UK. Most of the bands were American and of moderate popularity, yet still, the demands for their "riders" (all the food, drink and luxuries they might want for the day and night of the gig) were extortionate and often ran into tens of thousands of pounds of expense for the promoters. This was truly a waste of money – food and drink that would not get eaten but was there "just in case" and luxurious unnecessary equipment that also went unused, while extra assistants had to be paid just to run around after these pampered nincompoops. It may well have been money wasted but it was still accounted for in the budget and rarely ran over that because it was expected and planned for.

The point is, if you are spending your own money it is damned difficult to overspend in most businesses and football is no exception. It takes gross negligence and idiocy to run a previously solvent club into mountains of debt – in fact it is harder to do this than to run things effectively. The sheer amount of income generated by a football club should be enough to offset even the largest wage and tax demands – it is the extras where things generally go wrong. This is a book about the extras but also the nuts and bolts which should be solid when talking of football clubs in 2010. What has happened to the beautiful game and what can we do about it? Read on.

Paul Stenning, July 2010

1: THE BIGGEST TRANSFER FEE BLUNDERS

"Massimo Taibi is clearly a good keeper." – Roy Keane

Football as a whole is a subjective business. The majority of fans care not for the trophy-wielding prowess of their club, it's more about tradition, passion, commitment and belonging – quality on the pitch comes as a welcome bonus and if you win something, the Gods are smiling. Unless you're a fan of a top four side the chances are you can count on one hand the honours your team will have won in the last fifty years. But when you talk players there aren't enough fingers to dissect the opinions of good, bad, indifferent and downright terrible.

Most of the time football certainly comes down to subjectivity; these opinions and debates are what keeps the game ticking, what keeps fans busy and immersed in fanzines and online forums, not to mention the couple of hours before and after the game discussing the finer points of the left winger's lack of productivity.

However, every now and then there are business deals so gloweringly awful that there is suddenly no need for opinion – the deals were just bad, the player was not right for the club. Ultimately it is about profit. Clubs sign players either to help them win competitions which in turn will generate revenue, or they groom young players in order to sell on at a later stage when the player is hitting the height of their potential. Many smaller clubs, from Crewe to Brighton, have a long history of signing talented youngsters and selling them to bigger clubs. In the grand scheme of things the smaller clubs makes little of the player's true value, yet they make a very sizeable profit for a small club which is enough to re-invest in order to find another future talent.

Because the smaller clubs keep their risk level relatively low, they can rarely be accused of signing the proverbial turkey – a loss of £50,000 is always going to be recoverable even by clubs which may be ripe for administration. Although in relative terms this amount might equate to a mistake if the player turns out to be useless, it's certainly a greater problem for the bigger clubs who deal in millions – both in terms of transfer fees and the (often guaranteed) salary.

The biggest criticism of a player surely has to be if they were bought at a premium, did not perform on the pitch and were sold at a loss. This is inarguably bad investment. Quite often the biggest mistakes come when a player has made a move to the club of his dreams after performing well for a supposedly lesser side. Take the example of Garry Birtles. The striker had been a staple in the Nottingham Forest side guided by Brian Clough to an unprecedented two European Cups as well as a League Championship and two League Cups. Clough oversaw Birtles's move to Forest in 1977 when he negotiated a deal of £2,000 with non-league Long Eaton United, though Birtles was originally purchased as a winger. Initially it seemed as if the Nottingham native would be a mere fringe player as after a year and a half he had only made one appearance. Yet due to the sale of Peter Withe to Newcastle, Birtles received an unexpected chance to play up front against Liverpool in the European Cup. In just his third match for a professional side Birtles notched a goal and, from then on, his place in the Forest side was assured with a steady stream of goals following.

In total Birtles scored 32 goals in 87 appearances for the club and also appeared in an England shirt, but despite Forest's success during his four years at the club, Birtles yearned to pull on a Manchester United shirt and Forest did not turn down the £1.25m the Red Devils offered in 1980. They may have had the funds but at the time United did not have the success they were used to. After a prolonged injury crisis the club were desperate to improve and when they found themselves in mid-table, it was time to bring in a top striker.

That season United could finish only seventh and Garry Birtles was not exactly an instant success. Where he had an average of more than a goal every three games for Forest, he did not score for 30 games at Old Trafford. After 32 games he had scored just once. During this period United's management structure changed with the inevitable departure of Dave Sexton and the hiring of the enormously successful Ron Atkinson. Birtles did not feature in Atkinson's plans despite eventually notching 11 goals in his next 26 games for United. To Birtles's credit, he swallowed his pride and returned to the club where had made his name, enjoying another spell of success in the East Midlands. He would go on to play another 125 games for Forest, scoring 38 goals despite a spell where he played as a makeshift centre-half. For Nottingham Forest the Birtles saga was terrific business, selling a player who had already contributed to their most abundant period of trophy winning at a then impressive £1.25m. Less than two years later they bought the striker back for a paltry £300,000 where he again performed well for the club. For Manchester United, Birtles stands as one of their biggest transfer fee blunders, made at a time where the club was struggling as a whole.

It could be argued that perhaps United made an even bigger blunder twenty years later when they were being managed by the most successful gaffer in their history.

Billed as the replacement for the Danish giant Peter Schmeichel who had been one of United's best goalkeepers for some time, the Italian journeyman Massimo Taibi was unheralded and unheard of by fans. With Taibi's club Venezia receiving almost £4.5m for his services, it was understandably going to be difficult for Taibi to justify such a price tag and replace the heroic Schmeichel. On his debut for United, Taibi conceded two goals which a top level goalkeeper should have prevented. Bizarrely, however, perhaps because United won the match 3-2, he won the Man of the Match award.

Nevertheless the writing was on the wall very early on and despite retaining his place in the line-up Taibi again made an error the following week, conceding a sloppy goal to Wimbledon. Perhaps most memorably he let in three goals at home to Southampton, one of which was a stupidly slow shot from Matthew Le Tissier which just made it past the goal line. But it was the concession of a walloping five goals against Chelsea which sealed the Italian's fate. It was just the third time in 25 years that United had been on the end of such a drubbing. In less than a month Massimo Taibi had been put in his rightful place, at the helm of the Manchester United reserve squad where he stayed until a loan move to Reggina, ultimately resulting in a £2.5m purchase. United lost £2m in the Taibi fiasco but in this instance money was far outweighed by the indignity of such a poor goalkeeper representing a club of such eminence. Upon returning to Italy Taibi would score a goal at the end of a match against Udinese, earning his club a 1-1 draw. To his credit, he was not tainted by his experience or his

19

treatment in the press, preferring to look back on his time in the North West with fondness. In 2009 he told Goal.com, "When I speak of Manchester, I always remember the episodes against Liverpool. Emotions ... were unique, historic, and unparalleled."

When considering the vast number of signings made by Manchester United in their history it is no surprise that there are a great number of players who might be put forward as wasteful purchases. Yet most United fans would agree Juan Sebastian Veron would come close to top of the list for overrated and overhyped, not to mention overpriced. On 12 July 2001 Sir Alex Ferguson made a then record British purchase when he paid Lazio £28.1m for the services of Argentinian international midfielder Veron. Perhaps the price tag went to his head as, upon signing for the club, Veron was quoted as saying he had "no fear of the Premiership".

Perhaps not, but without respect for the league Veron was going to be in trouble. And so it would prove. Mindful of the enormous price tag looming over Veron's head, Sir Alex Ferguson was defensive over the early performances of the Argentinian, despite it appearing as if Veron was too slow and wooden to cope with the demands of the English top division.

By the end of the season United were staring a trophy-less season in the face for only the third time in 13 years. And Ferguson reacted with venom when, in particular, the merits of Veron were questioned by journalists in attendance at the team's training ground. Ferguson ordered the attendant throng to leave but not before unleashing a furious diatribe aimed at all of Veron's critics:

"I'm not fucking talking to you. He is a fucking great player," Ferguson said, his parting words ringing in the scribe's ears, "And you're all fucking idiots." In particular Ferguson seemed aggrieved at reports which claimed two of United's players confronted Veron after their Champions League exit to Bayer Leverkusen, blaming the hapless midfielder for several errors which had aided the Red Devils' exit. The United manager claimed it was "absolute nonsense, total lies". Voracious in his defence of Veron, the manager challenged the press to point out "what is wrong with Veron", Fergie believing his signing had "played well".

Yet, be it his questionable temperament, his lack of skill on the ball, a lack of goals and his oft questioned passing, Juan Sebastian Veron was destined to leave United, and leave them fast. For all the praise from his manager the facts remained: Veron cost United a record fee of £28.1m and made 75 appearances, scoring a meagre 11 goals. Two years after his arrival Veron was granted permission to speak with Chelsea about a move to Stamford Bridge and sure enough, despite United losing approximately £14m of their original investment, Veron wore blue for the 2003/04 season. His time at Chelsea was also poor and he made just 12 appearances for the club, spending more time on loan in Italy.

When it comes to strikers, the most damning evidence comes in terms of their goals to games ratio. The stats tend not to lie. Clearly, when talking Premier League standards, if a player manages thirty plus goals in a season they are something special. Only five players have managed this since the league's inception in 1992: Alan Shearer (who is also the league's top scorer by a ridiculously long way), Andy Cole, Kevin Phillips, Thierry Henry and Cristiano Ronaldo. It is no surprise that Henry, Cole and Shearer are the league's all time heaviest scorers.

In comparison, if a striker spends time at a club with a feeble goal ratio it must stand that the player was something of a wasteful purchase. If the player cost £7m in 1997 the statistic of 7 goals in 45 league games is genuinely alarming.

Stan Collymore signed for Liverpool in June 1995 for a then British record fee of £8.5 million. During his time at Anfield, Collymore had a record of a goal every other game, including two goals in a match many football fans remember as one of the best in the history of Sky Sports, the 4-3 spectacular where Liverpool got the better of Newcastle. Collymore was, according to the press, a part of the "Spice Boys", an unofficial Liverpool group of players who were accused of everything from hedonistic liaisons to wasting their natural football talent. Collymore often tried to distance himself from the group.

Something did not click with Collymore and Liverpool as he was sold to Aston Villa after just two seasons at Anfield where he certainly held a very respectable goalscoring record and even won three England caps. Liverpool lost £1.5m on their original investment which may seem unfortunate given that Collymore scored plenty of goals and helped the club to a respectable third place finish in the Premiership. Yet for Aston Villa, a £7m transfer fee represented a substantial outlay, a record for the club in fact.

Though Collymore would score both goals in Aston Villa's 2-1 victory over his former club Liverpool, as well as a hat-trick in Europe, mentally the striker was struggling. During a period of particularly poor form Collymore was admitted to the Priory Hospital in Roehampton where he was treated for clinical depression. Villa were not exactly sympathetic. Instead of supporting Collymore until he was back to performing his best for them, he was loaned out to Fulham where he only managed one goal. Ultimately, the striker was allowed to leave on a free transfer where he joined Leicester City. Though he had a few performances reminiscent of his best, Collymore's career was effectively over.

International football fans of a certain age may feel a certain fondness for the likes of Denmark's 1992 European championship winning side or the Cameroon side who sparked the World Cup to life in 1990. Similarly Romania have often provided entertainment in international matches and few can begrudge the fact that Gheorghe Hagi, Florin Răducioiu or Marius Lăcătuş were extremely good players who gave the Romanian side of the 1990s an elegant distinction. At Euro 2000 Romania had outgrown their classic players from a few years before and their striking hopes were pinned on Inter Milan's rising star Adrian Mutu, who was just 21.

The side reached the quarter-finals and Mutu made a strong impression. Though he failed to score in ten games for the *Nerazzurri*, Mutu remained in Italy and had successful spells at both Verona and Parma. In fact, his 18 goals in 31 league games for Parma led Chelsea to come calling for his services. Just two months after Roman Abramovich had bought the club, he was eager to display his financial clout and openly lavished millions on virtually anyone who was considered the current, or the next, big thing. Mutu was a little of both. He spoke to another former Romanian legend, one time Chelsea right back Dan Petrescu, who assured his compatriot that Chelsea would be a good move for him.

Mutu, who was from a poor background, considered the deal Chelsea made to be "too good to turn down". He was born in Arges County in southern Romania, an area known for its gypsy community and where the average annual wage is just over £4,000. With Chelsea, Mutu's annual gross salary now reached £2,350,000. Additionally he was rewarded with a signing on fee of £330,000 which was split into five instalments. Intriguingly Mutu's Romanian agent, Gigi Becali of Becali Sport SRL, was paid almost £100,000 more than Mutu for brokering the deal.

Chelsea signed the left-footer on a five-year deal and paid Parma £15.8m. Mutu became Abramovich's first new striker and the deal looked shrewd when Mutu scored four goals in his first three matches. His bright start for the club did not last, however, and as the season progressed he became less dynamic and scored fewer goals. By the time the new season rolled around and Chelsea hired new manager Jose Mourinho, there were frustrations brewing. Mourinho had not banked on the pride and passion Mutu would show for his country. "I don't care about being fined. I want everyone to know that the national team is the most important thing for me," Mutu told the BBC, regarding a public spat between the two. Mutu claimed Mourinho suggested he was injured when he wasn't in an attempt to stop him playing for Romania against the Czech Republic. He was also dropped from the Chelsea side with Mourinho producing a piece of paper that claimed the Romanian had a knee injury despite the striker claiming he was fully fit. Perhaps as a result of this apathy towards the new hierarchy at Chelsea Mutu was drug tested and found positive for cocaine. He was instantly sacked by the club. The FA hit him with a seven-month ban and a fine for £20,000.

After just 27 games and 6 goals for Chelsea, Adrian Mutu was now without a club and seemingly without much of a future. His goals cost a staggering £2.3m each. Unsurprisingly Chelsea sought to claim compensation on their shattered investment and after protracted court proceedings and costs, which of course they were also claiming for, Adrian Mutu was ordered to pay the club €17,173,990. By 2008 the player had not repaid any of the money due to his ongoing appeals and Chelsea were rewarded with a further windfall of 5 per cent interest p.a. on the outstanding balance. Despite this appeal system and his initial ban, Mutu returned to Italy where he began to perform on the pitch again, notching goals for Juventus and Fiorentina, most notably averaging a goal every 1.82 games for the latter. Sadly, however, Mutu twice failed doping tests in early 2010. On 10 January he was found to have the anti-obesity drug sibutramine in his system after playing for the Viola against Bari. Just ten days later after a match against Lazio, Mutu was again found to have the drug in his system. Italy's anti-doping prosecutor pressed for a one-year ban for the player, which seemed likely when Mutu admitted taking the drug. After an antidoping tribunal in April 2010 Mutu was banned from playing until the end of October 2010. The striker insisted he was "not happy" as the band seemed "excessive for a laxative."

Even Gigi Becali had to concede that should Mutu receive another ban his career would "be over". Given Fiorentina paid just €8m for a player who has certainly rewarded them on the pitch, financially they've not been too badly burned by Mutu's indiscretions (though it must be asked, why he continues to do such stupid things). And ultimately from Chelsea's point of view they would expect to be paid back at least a portion of the millions they handed to Adrian Mutu and his former club Parma. But when one thinks of graphic overspending and an abundance of financial waste one need look no further than a glorious talent who has thrown money down the drain in order to poison his body with drugs.

There are indeed countless examples of transfer fee blunders, and we can also view managers' entire tenures at particular clubs with financial disdain. One example would be Kevin Keegan's huge spending spree at Newcastle where he spent over £62m on players in five years with little financial return.

Hull City have also fallen foul of the "run before you can walk" syndrome within smaller clubs who find themselves promoted to the big time. Finding themselves on the precipice of relegation towards the end of the 2009/10 season, City chairman Adam Pearson blew his top over signings who had let the club down. It was in the striker department that Pearson felt the Tigers had been most useless and looking at the figures it was hard to disagree. Being £35m in debt, the club reasoned that their fruitless strikeforce had cost them a whopping £901,000 per goal scored. "We are spending £195,000 a week on strikers and between them they have scored just eight goals this season, which is not good enough," Pearson told The Sun. "We have the same annual wage bill as Sunderland but they have seven or eight young, saleable assets like Darren Bent, Kenwyne Jones, Fraizer Campbell and Craig Gordon. We don't have that. We have players on long contracts, high wages and no transfer value."

The club ultimately paid their strikers almost £8m in wages despite the meagre return. Jan Vennegoor of Hesselink was perhaps the most surprising given his European pedigree, the Dutchman scoring just 3 in 31 games. Jozy Altidore produced just 2 goals in 30 games while Kamel Ghilas scored just once in 16 outings. Both Amr Zaki and Daniel Cousin didn't even register a goal. At least Caleb Folan produced more consistent displays, with a slightly more creditable two goals from seven appearances.

Hull City are clearly a good example of a club that had limited reserves of spending. Because of this their manager's player purchases had to be exemplary in order for Hull to retain their Premier League status. On the flip side, Mark Hughes's reign at Manchester City was a blinding example of an exhaustive reserve of money leading to frivolous "kid in a sweet shop" spending. City's billionaire owner Sheikh Mansour bin Zayed Al Nahyan may have found the £100m Hughes spent in one spree inexpensive, but even by Premier League standards it was excessive. The ability to buy almost anyone who had the desire to be paid a lot of money (99 per cent of modern footballers, then) led to a dangerous precedent. For football's sake it was a positive outcome that Mark Hughes could only guide City to sixth place in the league and consequently lost his job. It is a very clear message that money alone does not guarantee success. Ironically it is those big clubs who seem to lose more money out of transfers than they recoup that are the most successful in terms of honours.

According to a piece which appeared in the *Munster Express*, between 1994 and 2005 three of the top English clubs spent and recouped the following on player transfers:

Chelsea
Spent £386m on 68 players; Made £84m on 84 players.
Avg. player in: £5.68m; Avg. player out: £1m.

Manchester United
Spent £229m on 41 players; Made £108m on 49 players.
Avg. player in: £5.58m; Avg. player out: £2.21m.

Arsenal
Spent £129m on 59 players; Made £92m on 103 players.
Avg. player in: £2.18m; Avg. player out: £0.89m.

With figures like these, is it any wonder that even the top clubs are in debt?

2: FOOTBALL AGENTS: A BUNG IN THE HAND

"Show me the money!" – Jerry Maguire

They may be a necessary evil in today's game yet the cost of football agents can certainly be deemed frivolous amongst the top clubs. It isn't just money that the agents cost clubs, or indeed players. But the sole purpose for the football agent tends to be exactly that – money. Even the good ones are in the job to get paid, why wouldn't they be? The really good ones enjoy the privilege of introducing a promising player to a club who goes on to be a terrific signing for the club, whether they made a return of £50,000 or £50m.

It is in fact the role of the agent which is one of the biggest changes to modern football, and one of the most irksome. There really is little point to the agent in many respects. The football association oversees their list of agents who are then licensed and allowed to deal with individual football league clubs. The role of the agent – as far as players are concerned – is said to be for the purpose of making sure that individual players' wants and needs are met. Whereas the FA, or even a trade union, could purport to overlook each individual transfer and each contract, they would not have the time or inclination to work so steadfastly for the player, especially those of a lower profile. This has led to an influx of agents who, while supposedly regulated, seem to develop a bad reputation from the media and players alike.

Perhaps, as we are led to believe, it is a minority of agents who give the rest a bad name. Yet would there really be so many individual cases of bungs and stealing players if agents were not, at some level, financially selfish and occasionally corrupt? Within the history of the game, football agents are a relatively phenomenon, appearing due to the Sky television takeover in the early 1990s. All of a sudden players were earning huge money, sportswear firms craved endorsement and transfer fees rocketed. Footballers became much more important as individuals than ever before. In the past, a football club was only as strong as the sum of its parts, it relied on the team ethic and the essence of team is as 11 individuals working as a whole. Transfer fees and salaries were realistic and reasonable in the 1980s. Few people would argue that the top stars of the 1950s, 60s and 70s deserved the relatively low wages they received. As entertainers, footballers have a right to be paid well and if this were the only purpose of an agent then it would not be a bad thing. But should an agent be paid anything from £5,000 to £100,000 for a few phone calls or for allowing his player to speak to a club? Some might argue that this is preposterous, but there are indeed agents who operate on this basis.

Even notwithstanding these types of obscene charges as well as the corruption alleged on the Panorama programme in 2006, agents still charge football clubs a ridiculous amount of money in the modern game – they are in fact one of the main creditors within any club's debt. According to Premier League figures, between October 2008 and September 2009, England's top-flight clubs spent more than £70m on agents' fees. The list is as follows:

Manchester City	£12,874,283
Chelsea	£9,562,223
Liverpool	£6,657,305
Tottenham	£6,066,935
West Ham	£5,527,548
Arsenal	£4,760,241
Wigan	£3,576,972
Portsmouth	£3,184,725
Bolton	£3,166,611
Everton	£2,008,407
Sunderland	£2,007,040
Aston Villa	£1,708,374
Blackburn	£1,610,885
Hull	£1,599,188
Manchester United	£1,517,393
Fulham	£1,469,258
Wolves	£1,235,703
Birmingham	£974,982
Stoke	£716,042
Burnley	£468,398

During this period Mark Hughes spent a ludicrous £150m in the transfer market. Manchester City purchased Emmanuel Adebayor and Joleon Lescott for a combined total of £47.5m, and they also splurged on goalkeeper Shay Given, defenders Wayne Bridge and Kolo Toure, strikers Craig Bellamy, Carlos Tevez and Roque Santa Cruz as well as midfielders Gareth Barry and Nigel de Jong. Even these were not the sum of City's total spend. City chief financial officer Graham Wallace told the club's website, "The figure in question relates to payments made for 35 players, many of whom predate this time period. The fees represent an average of £360,000 paid to agents per transaction, and the total amount falls well within our annual budget and operating plan as approved by our board."

Sheikh Mansour bin Zayed Al Nahyan, the multi-billionaire owner of the club, is clearly in a position to absorb such excessive fees to those who rate as nothing more than middle men, but does it represent value for money? How can it, when we are talking about such world-class players? They alone are in a position to negotiate the best deal given they are going to find a club willing to pay what they believe they are worth in this day and age. Is the agent really necessary? The quick answer would of course be no, but the truth is perhaps sketchier than this. Despite the City manager of the time, Mark Hughes, receiving criticism for his "defending" of the club's immense spending spree, it has to be noted that Hughes was realistic in his summation of the football agent's role and indeed, necessity. "There is a role that has to be met and, at the moment, agents fill it," Hughes said. "Do they provide value for money? You have to base every deal on its merits. Sometimes you feel the agent has really done his job, on others you feel he is getting money for nothing." This, perhaps, is the best analysis of the modern football agent – some are good, some are bad. Some make the effort to truly represent their client and take their payments as being relative to the work put in on behalf of a player earning millions, others are there for nothing more than to line their pockets for as little as possible.

There is a firm belief amongst the less successful managers that more is better, that a player's reputation can justify excessive spending. When the likes of Wigan have to shell out £3,576,972 for players who are listed as "free" it calls into question the validity of the system and further highlights superfluous overspending regarding agents.

An agent's cut on average is around 7 to 8 per cent of the transfer fee but in some cases this can be more like 25 to 30 per cent, or even higher. Alex

Levack, who represents City's Micah Richards, explains an agent's role:

> "I think it depends on the individual or the company
> they're employed by [he said]. Some agents are happy to
> just do the football deal and some agents literally manage
> everything off the pitch whether it be finances, buying
> a house, car, mobile phone, going on holiday. I think
> it also depends on the player's preference: some players
> want you to do all of that and others don't. I think you've
> got to bespoke it for each individual client."

Agents' fees and their job descriptions are now under greater scrutiny than
ever before. The publishing of the figures paid by the top clubs to agents was
the first time these had ever been revealed publicly. Under new regulations,
clubs had to agree to the publication of the figures.

What the figures will not show, however, is the illicit dealings from
certain agents at the behest of securing certain players who they desperately
wanted on their books. In many cases these are young "promising" players
who have yet to be signed by any club. One source explains:

> "There are kids as young as seven and eight being tapped
> up by agents, with their parents being offered big sums
> of money to sign contracts which basically mean the
> kid will stay with that agent until they go with a club
> that will pay a certain amount of money for the player's
> services. As soon as a club signs that kid, whether he is
> 12 or 17, that agent will have the document that says he
> should take a percentage of the deal."

By the time a player is 18, if he has any potential whatsoever then the
likelihood is he will already have an agent. But in this instance, the more
bloodthirsty agents will not be put off by the fact a player is already
represented by someone else. Agent Barry Silkman says:

> "A lot of agents out there are not what I would call
> nice people. There are a lot of agents that will approach

players that are already under contract to other agents and entice them to leave their agents, something which I have never done, or ever would do. It doesn't interest me. Generally, it is not a great game to be in."

Silkman, however, can hardly be called a nice person himself. In 2001 he sued Newcastle United over the transfer of Chilean midfielder Clarence Acuna. Silkman was recorded unbeknownst to him where he revealed the reason for his anger. The tape ran:

> "I got fucked by Newcastle and I ended up taking them to court. I settled for 25 grand when they owed me 100 grand. I took a player [Acuna] there [Newcastle] on trial. His club wanted £2.5m but I said don't pay it because they have got to sell the player. He ended up signing for 900 grand and yet they [Newcastle] still fucked me. Bobby Robson was my first manager at Fulham. I'd always kept in contact and I said 'Bob how could you let them fuck me?' You know what he said? 'You don't count. I'm the only one that counts. That's your hard luck.' So you know what I said to him? I said: 'I have a wife and a young daughter and a fucking mortgage and you've turned round and said that to me'. I said: 'See that cancer on your nose? I hope it spreads all over your face and that you live a fucking long, long, long life because the longer you live the more you will fucking suffer.'"

Silkman was clearly enraged and almost psychopathic, telling Robson:

> "There's only one God and he's looking down at us two now and he's saying 'Whose side am I on?' And let me tell you, Bob, it ain't fucking yours because I have never fucked anyone in my life. Fuck knows how many people you have fucked', and I walked out."

Silkman had been in negotiations with then Newcastle chairman Freddy

Shepherd over his commission on the Acuna deal. He explained:

> "Freddy Shepherd came on the phone to me and went over the deal with me. I said: 'Do I get it in writing?' and he said, "Yes, you will have it in writing." When I went to the lawyer ... I had it all on tape. I sent the tape to a journalist, 17 minutes and 18 seconds of him [Shepherd] saying to me: "I will never do you up, I will always look after you, I'm not that type of person. If we are going to sign the player I promise you, I guarantee you, you will get paid." I had the conversation on the Saturday morning and they signed him on the Tuesday. I took him there on trial, I paid for everything but they never even offered me the money I had laid out."

It was a rare moment of club power overtaking that of the agent who, let's face it, does no favour to the club themselves. An agent is linked to the player, they provide no service to a club other than that usually of an irritant and a necessary evil. Considering agents fight amongst themselves, what chance do the clubs and players have to conduct sensible, respectful business dealings? Even Silkman, who denies that football agents are in any way corrupt, says, "What I would say is that there are a lot of agents out there who will virtually do anything within their power to steal a player away from another agent."

In 2006, then Luton Town manager Mike Newell made public a claim that during the January transfer window he had personally been offered bungs by several agents. One of these agents was caught on film in a *Panorama* special programme on corruption in football. The agent himself claimed on camera that corruption was widespread among clubs and that certain managers accepted "bungs".

The agent, who was not named for legal reasons (but who Newell later revealed as Charles Collymore, no relation to Stan), told *Panorama* investigators, "There's managers out there who take bungs all day long. (Name deleted), you know that, takes bungs all day long. We've got (name deleted) FC, yep, all day long." Later in the filming, most controversially he revealed, "I would say to you comfortably there's six to eight managers we could definitely approach and they'd be up for this, no problem."

Mike Newell's comments were the most revealing, given he was in charge of a well established football institution in Luton. Likewise, Newell was a model professional player and had no benefit in coming out with the allegations, in fact it strongly damaged his career. After his comments and the subsequent media furore – including an appearance on the BBC *Ten O'Clock News* – it seems it was Newell who suffered most. After making comments which were considered sexist about a female referee whilst still at Luton, Newell soon found himself looking for a new club. He kept Grimsby Town in the football league but was relieved of his duties after just a year at Blundell Park. Since then he has not returned to football. Charles Collymore, however, is still an active football agent. Almost three years after the *Panorama* programme aired he was cleared by the FA who said they could not prove any allegations against him. Collymore was accused of touting Enoch Showunmi to Millwall while he was still registered as a Luton player and also having a "sham arrangement" with an unlicensed agent during Showunmi's subsequent transfer to Bristol City. Newell claimed he was offered money by former footballer Mark Wilson who was working with Collymore to broker a deal for Showunmi. The player himself was fined £2,000 for later using Wilson to help negotiate his transfer to Bristol City. The Bristol club were fined £15,000 for using Wilson and making no attempt to find out if he was a licensed agent.

"It really disappoints me when I hear people saying that money paid to agents is going out of the game," Collymore said, after his name was cleared. "More should be done to recognise agents as legitimate members of the football family. This industry is never going to be popular. We're like estate agents. I can't speak for everybody but I can say that 99 per cent of us run a decent, honest business."

Other high profile figures, however, felt differently. In an interview with the *News of the World*, Sven-Goran Eriksson claimed that three unnamed Premier League clubs were riddled with corruption and regularly made illegal payments in respect of transfer deals. Crucially, in the *Panorama* programme, two high profile Premiership managers were implicated in shady business dealings. The coup in the programme was the revelation that both Sam Allardyce and Harry Redknapp were apt for bungs. Agent Teni Yerima said he bribed Bolton manager Allardyce and another agent, Peter Harrison, claimed he paid Mr Allardyce's son Craig to secure deals with Bolton. In the film,

Craig Allardyce was seen boasting about access to his father. Sam Allardyce told the BBC he had never taken, asked for, or received a bung.

Harry Redknapp was secretly filmed, allegedly "tapping up" Blackburn's Andy Todd, through an agent. Redknapp, however, claimed he was "a million per cent innocent" and had never taken any bungs.

An inquiry was launched to investigate the claims within the programme and the further claims that resulted from Mike Newell's comments. The Stevens Inquiry was headed by Lord Stevens but as is so often the case in investigations of this sort, the report found very little and proved largely inconclusive. There were no charges brought against Allardyce or Redknapp. In fact, bizarrely, it was only Luton Town who suffered. They received a points deduction and were fined after breaching FA rules. Given Stevens has written for *News of the World*, and claims were made within the exact same newspaper, couldn't there have said to be a conflict of interest? Lord Stevens was also responsible for the farcical report into Princess Diana's death which found no evidence of any truth in the conspiracy theories surrounding her death, despite evidence to the contrary.

Despite investigating 17 player transfers, involving five clubs, three managers and numerous agents and other third parties, Stevens's report stated: "There is no evidence of any irregular payments to club officials or players, and they are identified only as a consequence of the outstanding issues the inquiry has with the agents involved".

It seems rather implausible that there is no corruption within the game, especially concerning agents, but football fans are expected to get excited over revelations which ultimately are always unfounded. Those in the highest positions of the game are apt to protect those directly beneath them, and as is often the case the managers who are often accused of corruption, such as Redknapp, manage to escape unscathed.

Agents almost seem to be protective over their relationships with managers, though it is certainly possible that they could be telling the truth when defending those whom they have had business relationships with. Former footballer Lee Payne, who features Stephen Ireland, Ben Foster and Paddy Kenny on his books, says:

> "I've been in this business for ten years and I keep a clean
> ship. I'm far from alone. I've dealt with Sam Allardyce

and he was very professional. There was never a question of him wanting to be 'looked after'. I've done deals with Harry Redknapp, too – I helped take Svetoslav Todorov to West Ham and then Portsmouth – and, again, he was a joy to work with. There was never a question of a bung. But sadly, some agents give us all a bad name."

Payne, however, does hint that it is not squeaky clean behind the scenes and he reveals his disgust for the scenes within the *Panorama* programme:

"I'm proud of my job and I feel privileged to be involved in football. I've nothing to be ashamed about. But I watched *Panorama* and I was disgusted, absolutely disgusted. It sickened me, although it didn't surprise me. Only the naive would believe bungs don't happen in football. Me? I'm not naive. I know of agents who will be thinking: 'Thank God these *Panorama* investigators never approached me'. I know what goes on, I just try to avoid it. Deals are done and I think: 'How on earth has that happened? How can he have ended up going there?' Then I realise: 'Oh, it's the manager's agent at work.'"

Payne played for the likes of Newcastle and Reading, as well as spending six years in the Netherlands before injury finished his career. His father was also a manager of a non-league outfit and Payne reveals, "When I stand opposite a chief executive and we talk business, I feel like I've earned the right to be there. But I look at some agents and I wonder what right they have to be involved. These people have no football background, they were probably selling double glazing last year."

Payne is right of course. The advancing of agents – the sheer numbers and the sheer greed of those who are desperate to find anyone who may turn out to be a money spinner – has enabled those with no football background to become involved and make themselves money. It is no surprise given that even the clubs themselves are often owned by businessmen with little knowledge or experience from within the game.

It wasn't always like this, however. Pini Zahavi is now the godfather of football agents, and though he may have been involved in many unsavoury incidents within the game, his beginnings were certainly more about the love of football. However, a chance deal made Zahavi realise he was onto something.

Pinhas Zahavi was born in Nes Ziona, a small town close to Tel Aviv, in 1955. The Zahavi family did not have to worry about money when Pini was growing up; among his siblings is a brother who is a successful heart surgeon. Pini attended primary school with Jacob Shahar who today owns Israeli side Maccabi Haifa. But it was with Maccabi Tel Aviv that Zahavi was to make his first profit from football. He had made several contacts in the game during the 1974 World Cup, which was held in West Germany. It was an unusual World Cup given England did not qualify but Scotland did. It was because of Scotland's appearance that Zahavi – who attended the tournament behind the scenes in order to network – met and befriended the likes of Graeme Souness and Kenny Dalglish. Souness would come in very handy when, five years after the World Cup, he initiated contact between Zahavi and then Liverpool manager Bob Paisley. Paisley was interested in Israeli defender Avi Cohen of Maccabi Tel Aviv, who would eventually sign for Liverpool for £200,000. Zahavi took a small portion of the fee and the first signs were clear that there was money to be had for third parties involved in football transfers. "It was nothing like now," Zahavi would later say. "Then I only loved football. But that deal showed me how you could make some money from the game. I think it was the real start of the agents."

It would take several years for Zahavi to emerge as a serious player in the football world, but through his burgeoning contacts, Zahavi began to become involved in the English game. He counts the likes of Ron Atkinson and Terry Venables as close friends. In 2010 Zahavi is even closer to the current crop of Premier League managers. His first real coup came when he spotted a young Rio Ferdinand playing for West Ham in 1997 after he had brokered a deal for Eyal Berkovic, who joined the Hammers from Southampton. Five years later Zahavi oversaw Ferdinand's hefty £30m transfer from Leeds United to Manchester United. There was controversy when Ferdinand was photographed in a London restaurant with Zahavi and Chelsea's Peter Kenyon at a time when his United contract was up for renewal. Zahavi later said the meeting was "totally innocent". He was also implicated regarding secret meetings with representatives of Chelsea involving Sven-Goran Eriksson, in July 2003. Eriksson was filmed meeting with Roman Abramovich whilst still England manager.

Zahavi represents the modern world of football agents, having been involved with a large degree of controversy, yet seemingly always managing to emerge unscathed. Today he still represents Ferdinand, who earns a fortune from both his Manchester United wages, which are in the region of £150,000 a week, and multiple sponsorship deals. He is also the agent for Everton striker Yakubu, who began his senior career with Maccabi Haifa. The Nigerian eventually moved to Portsmouth before joining Middlesbrough in a £7.5m deal which earned Pini Zahavi the biggest football agent's fee ever recorded, a whopping £3 million.

Yet Zahavi's business dealings do not end with personal profit. He is a market leader in the business of third party ownership. When Argentinian internationals Carlos Tevez and Javier Mascherano arrived at West Ham, many could smell a rat and it turned out to be a disastrous scenario, though Zahavi again would not lose out in any way. Zahavi acts as a broker for Media Sports Investment (MSI), the company which owned both Tevez and Mascherano. Kiavash Joorabchian made the news as he was the front for the company but the deal was principally manufactured by Zahavi. Both players of course were South American and within South America the model of third party ownership has long been standard practice.

MSI made £5m in agent fees when the Argentinians joined West Ham but there was also a clause in the contract which essentially forced the Hammers to sell both players within five years, as it was written that they would have to sell either or both if an offer over a certain amount was made. This sell-on transfer fee would also carry with it a further agent's fee for MSI. If West Ham had wanted to keep both Tevez and Mascherano they would have had to pay MSI £40 million. This kind of deal is increasingly common, thanks to Zahavi, but it is something that is unsustainable for the majority of football clubs. West Ham would not have been sensible to spend £40m on two players but Zahavi knew that both were so good there were bound to be offers over £5m for each of them individually. It was an agent's coup which did nothing for the good name of football.

Ultimately West Ham lost out by being fined for breaking rules regarding third party ownership, though Kia Joorabchian still kept a place at the club, working as a "transfer advisor" as late as 2009. Though Mascherano would eventually move to Liverpool in a deal worth over £18million it was again MSI, and not West Ham, who profited. Unable to keep up the wage payments to Mascherano and burned by the bad press the deal had affected, West Ham loaned Mascherano out to Liverpool and all MSI had to do was to simply wait until he was out of his contract with West Ham in order to pick up the sell-on fee.

The situation was much the same with Carlos Tevez, although this brought about extra controversy. Tevez's goals were a determining factor in West Ham retaining their Premier League status in the 2006/07 season, and Sheffield United were relegated in their place, causing a long series of appeals from the Yorkshire club who were eventually rewarded £20m compensation.

Tevez meanwhile moved to Manchester United on loan until he was out of contract with West Ham. Although United were willing to pay MSI £25.5m for his services, the Argentinian felt his position at Old Trafford was untenable and opted to move to bitter rivals Man City. The eventual transfer fee was not officially disclosed but it was rumoured to be around £47m, a cost both the club and MSI denied. Regardless, it is safe to say that from the sell-on fees for just two players, Pini Zahavi and Kia Joorabchian would have made a small fortune. Joorabchian in fact personally represents more than sixty players throughout the world. Though Manchester City and Liverpool currently "own" the two South American players, it is only for the duration of the contract, which means essentially that unless both renegotiate new deals, their current clubs will have paid for their services only for the duration of their contracts. Ultimately this is one very expensive loan deal.

Zahavi is the perfect representation of the modern football agent, and indeed the game in general. He is not satisfied with his own multi-million pound fortune amassed from high profile transfer deals, but rather he is aggressively pursuant in making more and more money from various ventures, his desire for wealth seemingly unquenchable. It is no longer for the love of the game but for the love of wealth that Zahavi operates. But, given his power within the game, it can only have a negative knock on effect for those football clubs he chooses to deal with.

Zahavi is the sole consultant to the Hero Football Fund, set up this summer. Committee members include former Liverpool footballer Alan

Hansen (whom Zahavi had again forged a bond with at the 1974 World Cup), former Premiership referee David Elleray and QC David Griffith-Jones, who specialises in sports law. The company procures wealthy individuals by way of promising them a future 10 per cent minimum profit on their investment. Individuals have been asked to contribute a minimum of $100,000 into the fund, and belief came from powerful quarters, with the national bank of Dubai spilling £27m of their own money into the fund, which aims to make profit from footballers' "economic rights", a phrase which Pini Zahavi has long exploited. This can be anything from a player's "image" to their "brand".

The aim of the fund is said to include helping smaller clubs, yet it is difficult to see exactly how clubs will benefit from such deals. Ultimately it is all about making independent organisations a huge amount of money off the back of players, something which should surely remain with a player's club.

Individual agents can be problematic for their players, and they do not always do the right and proper thing on behalf of their client. Agent Alex Levack says, "There still are agents who do take advantage of their clients. In a lot of industries when bad things happen, people are very quick to jump on the negatives."

One of the most glaring examples of taking advantage of a client came when agent Ian Elliott was charged and arrested under fraud allegations. It came when his client, Middlesbrough winger Stewart Downing, claimed that up to £500,000 of his earnings had vanished. Over a period of 15 months Downing had become suspicious that his earnings from commercial deals had seemingly disappeared. Elliott had been another character who almost appeared on the *Panorama* programme, having been offered £1.2m by the bogus business man who wished to buy his clients. He pulled out of the programme at the last minute, sensing something was not quite right. But Elliot would later claim to the press, "I've not been offered a bung or offered a bung in 20 years in football." Three years after the programme Elliott found himself charged on five counts of fraud relating to Stewart Downing. He lost the England player as a consequence and the charges are still unresolved.

It isn't just the agents of course. There has to be someone with power to bung and that often means a chairman or a manager. This was made clear with the charges brought against former Hull City chairman Paul Duffen, whom the club claimed had bunged or been bunged by agents regarding certain business deals.

City alleged that agents, who are not named, paid bungs to Duffen via Reef Securities, a company registered in the Bahamas with an office in Guernsey. Duffen denied all the charges. He was also accused of spending less time at the ground than he should and claiming personal expenses which were far and beyond those he was entitled to as chairman. Hull were certainly in dire straits, having spent far too much on players at the behest of remaining a Premier League club, and they were relegated in the 2009/10 season. Part of their overall debt concerned deals with agents. Hull were obliged to pay £4.5m in agents' fees over a 12-month period. Duffen's brief association with the club, where he certainly did more harm than good, was a sad reflection on the current state of club ownership. Duffen, a Tottenham fan, had previously attempted and failed to buy both West Ham United and Cardiff City. Hull were seemingly a lowly third on the list, or perhaps they were the only club naive enough to be convinced by the millionaire status of Duffen and his consortium. He made promises which he certainly kept in terms of buying expensive, quality players; the only problem was neither he or Hull City could keep up the payments to players or indeed agents.

Many agents will deny they are in any way harmful to the game and that they only take what is rightfully theirs. If they broker a deal they can expect to be paid the same way an Independent Financial Advisor would. To an extent there is nothing wrong with this entitlement. Of course, any person who does a job for a player, as well as the club, should be paid for their work in making a deal happen. No one in football would begrudge the moral right to be paid for work completed. What is often distasteful is the sheer greed of most agents involved in the game; witness the tirade launched by Barry Silkman, or indeed the allegations against Ian Elliot. The truth is, however, that these are mere dots on the landscape of corruption and gluttony. The real power comes in the form of super agents like Pini Zahavi who has cleverly orchestrated the opportunity for both himself and other agents to flourish, sometimes at the expense of the clubs involved. Zahavi has become so powerful that he is likely to be credited with reducing a football club's ability to hold on to its most powerful assets – their players.

If, as will most certainly become the case (and already has in Zahavi's dealings), a football club's hands are tied with regards to the ownership of its players, then that club no longer has any power, it is yielded to the super agent or his company. All star players would be on glorified loans to clubs and only Zahavi and the player himself would profit in the long-term. It then prompts the inevitable likelihood that clubs will no longer be able to afford to pay either their players or the agents and become further and further indebted. If they are then not successful on the pitch with their starting loanee 11, they are destined for lower league finishes and ultimately, administration. Once again, we revert to the familiar argument regarding football agents – can they really be any good for the game?

Sources: *Guardian, Independent, The Sun, News of the World,* BBC, The FA, *Paul Stenning interviews, www.sport.co.uk*

WASTE OF MONEY!

3: THE RIDSDALE SAGA

"Clubs are better for being run on business principles because it does mean that decisions taken are considered rather than emotional." – Peter Ridsdale

Club chairmen have a thankless task in many ways. On paper their job is not necessarily demanding; if they inherit a stable financial situation they are merely overseeing the basic day to day running of the club without the managerial pressure of winning game after game. Indeed the hardest decision might just be whether to keep faith with a losing manager or in negotiating the arrival of a new, talented coach. As with football itself, however, paper never tells the full story and things are much easier in theory. One wrong decision as chairman can lead to a negative domino effect that can endanger the history and tradition of even the longest standing, strongest clubs.

When Peter Ridsdale became chairman at Leeds United it was a dream vocation, taking charge of club affairs for the team he loved. Robert Peter Ridsdale was born 11 March 1952 in Leeds and the club was in his blood. Ridsdale was a season ticket holder from the age of ten. In 1965 (the days when tickets were only available from queuing at the club box office), the 13-year-old Yorkshireman spent the night in a sleeping bag outside Elland Road to ensure he got tickets for the FA Cup Final, which Leeds lost 2-1 to Liverpool. Even when working in Cardiff, Ridsdale still owned a home on the edge of the Yorkshire Dales with his second wife, Sophie, and their two children. Ridsdale's four sons from a previous marriage are all staunch Leeds supporters.

Ridsdale's hero when he was growing up was goalkeeper Gary Sprake, a character who drew admiration and scorn in equal measure, the time he threw the ball in his own net probably doing little to underline his reputation as a Leeds legend. But as a young keeper himself, who played in goal for

Yorkshire, Ridsdale certainly looked up to the Welsh international. Perhaps prophetically, Sprake's time at Leeds was, according to a former team-mate, characterised by "women, drinking and fighting". Leeds of course earned a reputation as the team everyone loved to hate and despite doing much to lose this tag after the end of the 1970s, by the time Peter Ridsdale took over as chairman of the club, the reputation was soon to be restored.

Ridsdale's business acumen was well known in the retail industry by the time he was in his thirties and he excelled as the chief executive of the clothing chains Sock Shop and Jumpers. His connections to Leeds remained, however, and his real desire was to work within the football industry. After a spell working for the Burton clothing chain as managing director he got the chance to work at Leeds United, as Burton was then one of the club's sponsors.

An article on the BBC website suggests that Ridsdale was seen as being a "puppet" to the owners of Leeds Sporting, a "suit" who may have been biting off more than he could chew. The truth of the matter, however, is that Leeds Sporting was practically Ridsdale's company, which he operated as managing director, overseeing 155 employees.

In April of 1999 Leeds Sporting announced a £1.86m half-year profit, but Ridsdale cryptically issued a warning that in order for most football clubs to survive, spiralling wages and transfer fees had to be brought under control. At the same time he offered then manager David O'Leary a new five-year contract worth £6m. However, Ridsdale showed a true lack of footballing knowhow when he claimed in the press that O'Leary had a job at Leeds "for life". Showing equally poor judgement, Ridsdale gave an interview where he referred to the legendary Don Revie's Leeds side as being "talented nearly-men", insinuating his current crop of players were about to outshine their 1970s predecessors.

Though Leeds were initially successful during Ridsdale's tenure, behind the scenes things were much more worrying. Midfielder Lee Bowyer and defender Jonathan Woodgate were involved in front page headlines after they were both involved in an incident which left an Asian student hospitalised with severe injuries. Bowyer was cleared of any wrongdoing but Woodgate was found guilty of affray and sentenced to community service.

Despite the off-field controversy, that season Leeds reached their first semi-final in European competition for 25 years where they met Turkish giants Galatasaray in the semi-final of the Uefa Cup.

At this time, Ridsdale also announced that Leeds Sporting's profits had risen by 89 per cent in the last six months of 2000. The financial future for Leeds, if nothing else, looked decidedly bright.

The Galatasaray match itself, which Leeds lost over both legs, was overshadowed by the death of two Leeds fans who were stabbed to death. Before he finally succumbed to his injuries Christopher Loftus was visited by Ridsdale in Taksim hospital. The chairman was described as "visibly upset" and he spoke with incredulity when approached by reporters. "It is a tragedy," Ridsdale said. "One minute I was talking to Galatasaray directors to promote the friendship between the two clubs and the next minute I receive a telephone call telling me there had been some problems in town and a fan had been killed."

In a BBC report the Leeds chairman was commended for his behaviour during both the Woodgate/Bowyer incident and tragedy in Turkey, two very unsavoury occurrences in Leeds's history. The reporter indicated that, "Peter Ridsdale has managed to tiptoe through a diplomatic minefield with dignity and restraint." This had certainly been the case and it was clear that as a lifelong supporter Ridsdale felt just as much of the impact from the death of two Leeds fans and would rightly have felt dismayed at the behaviour of two of his senior players. Additionally Ridsdale sought to make himself approachable for all supporters of the club, investigating their complaints about poor treatment and conditions, whether this was at Elland Road or away grounds. Ridsdale insisted that he was the supporters' representative on the Leeds United board. He was, however, beginning to develop a reputation for exaggeration and untrustworthiness. Days before signing Mark Viduka in a £7m purchase from Celtic, Ridsdale had insisted the club were not interested in the Australian international.

In the 2000/01 season Leeds again reached the semi-final stages in Europe, this time in the European Cup, where they were defeated by Valencia. The competition was a guaranteed money spinner due to TV rights and sponsorship but it depended on qualifying regularly for the competition. Despite their strong squad, Leeds invested in a new captain, purchasing West Ham's central defender Rio Ferdinand for £18m, breaking their existing transfer record. In order to fund this and other purchases, including Robbie Fowler and Seth Johnson (who, incidentally, Ridsdale had also claimed the club were not interested in purchasing), Ridsdale administered a £60m loan for the club. This was at the behest of Leeds United qualifying for the Champions League the next season and receiving hefty future gate receipts and the requisite sponsorship money. The next season, however, Leeds failed to qualify for the competition, finishing fifth in the Premiership.

Yet the signs of financial difficulties were clear enough even during this period. After their previous few years of profit it was surprising to see Leeds Sporting announce, in March 2001, that their profits for 2000 had fallen by 99 per cent due to the purchases of a number of high cost players. The question had to be, given that Leeds had enjoyed an unprecedented run of success with mostly young, inexpensive players, why were they now going for broke in order to strengthen their squad? Presumably Ridsdale had designs on winning the Premiership and the Champions League. Just one of these competitions would have been a terrific return for a Leeds side whose last major honour came in 1991/92 when they had won the First division. Instead, Ridsdale's lust for club triumphs (and let's be honest, it was probably as much to do with wanting unparalleled success for his boyhood club rather than mere financial profit) led Leeds down a dead end street. Unless they could at least qualify for the Champions League, it would not matter who was on their books.

2001 was perhaps the beginning in the downturn of Ridsdale's reputation. Several Leeds players were part of a Players Association' planned strike concerning a dispute over television money. Ridsdale kindly informed any players who were thinking of striking that if they did so they would not be paid any wages. During this period Ridsdale was also negotiating a move away from Elland Road, which seemed inconceivable from a staunch supporter and angered the entire populous of Leeds United fans who responded with vicious hate mail. He had also been bombarded with angry letters at the conclusion of the Bowyer-Woodgate trial, largely because he had kept faith with both players. Strictly speaking Ridsdale had not gone against his promises made at the time of the trial. The chairman had promised that if either player was found guilty of assault then they would be swiftly sacked by the club. Found guilty of only affray, Woodgate just escaped due to this lamentable distinction.

Many felt as if the mere association of violence with two high profile footballers should have been enough for the chairman to act in finding them a new employer. After a 0-0 draw with Everton at Goodison Park in March, Ridsdale marched down the touchline to confront the away fans who had been chanting abuse aimed in his direction for the majority of the match. Sensing a potentially high profile, unsavoury incident, the FA and police stepped in to warn the Leeds chairman he would be arrested if he ever made such a gesture again. The same month Leeds United's finances again came under scrutiny when it was announced they had lost £13.8m in the last six months of 2000.

Though the Whites made a quick turnaround and profit on the sale of Rio Ferdinand, who joined Manchester United for £30m in July 2002, it hinted at financial problems. Leeds should have been building the squad for successive European appearances and continual pressure on the big four at the top of the Premiership. Instead they were selling their biggest asset. Manager David O'Leary, who had guided Leeds to some of their best performances and success for a quarter of a century, was extremely opposed to the sale of Ferdinand, reasoning if Leeds were to continue their spell as one of the top English sides, they had to maintain their prized players, not sell them on. Peter Ridsdale thought otherwise, though the chairman also knew the full extent of Leeds's financial plight. In short, to all outsiders, the figures didn't add up.

Despite their European success and a prolonged spell at the heights of the Premiership Leeds were amassing worrying debts and no one aside from Peter Ridsdale seemed to know about it. Despite the insertion of trusted football steward Terry Venables, Leeds were destined to plunge further down the table as they were being forced to sell their most valuable players, most notably Jonathan Woodgate whom, Ridsdale had promised Venables, would definitely not be sold. Additionally, the former England manager saw other prized assets walking out of Elland Road including another fairly recent acquisition in Robbie Fowler. Veteran keeper Nigel Martyn, flair winger Harry Kewell, ever improving striker Robbie Keane and Lee Bowyer also left the club.

The 2002/03 season saw the end of Leeds's successful run in both England and Europe when they finished a disappointing 15th in the league, despite Mark Viduka's 20 goals.

Ridsdale resigned from the Leeds board, suggesting his tenure at the club was almost over, and sure enough insolvency specialist (a grim clue) Gerald

Krasner took over the club's affairs at the end of March 2003 with the true extent of Leeds's debts yet to be revealed. Coming at the end of the financial year, March had long been a pertinent month for Peter Ridsdale and it was ironic, perhaps bittersweet, that he chose this date to leave the club.

The Ridsdale saga had unavoidably penetrated Leeds inside and out, and the club, badly wounded from the bulk of its squad being dismantled, failed to even retain its Premiership status. In the 2003/04 season Leeds were relegated after finishing second from bottom. That year Mark Viduka scored 11 goals. Arsenal went the season undefeated while Leeds lost 21 games and had a goal difference of minus 39.

It was financially, however, where Leeds were really suffering. The figures were sketchy, the information behind the figures sketchier still, but it was announced that Leeds United, after just a few years with Ridsdale in control of the club, were in debt to the tune of £103m. The press were incredulous, taking stock of the chairman's office and calculating even the relaxing pastime of fish-keeping was costing the club £200 a year in maintenance, a revelation Ridsdale predictably opposed, reasoning the club had been turning over £86m a year at the time. "It's like, excuse me – go to the PFA headquarters, what have they got in reception? They have got a goldfish tank," he said.

Naturally, Ridsdale was often questioned about his involvement with the club and just how he managed to bring the club into so much debt. He denied much of the responsibility, putting it down to performances on the pitch (had Leeds qualified for the Champions League again, he reasoned, then they would have managed to repay the vast borrowings allocated for transfer fees).

"I have no insight into their financial affairs now," Ridsdale told Radio 5 Live. "What I do know is that when I left Leeds four years ago they had Paul Robinson, Harry Kewell, Mark Viduka and Alan Smith, among others. That team should never have been relegated, never mind finding themselves in the plight they are now." Ridsdale was referring to the fact Leeds had dropped down two divisions since his time at the club and were seemingly in limbo, unable to attract big name players to the club and mindful of having to sell lucrative assets such as their 2009/10 top scorer Jermaine Beckford who eventually joined Everton on a free transfer after attracting interest from several Premier League clubs.

"They have got to regroup now," Ridsdale continued unabated. "They are a very big club off the field but what matters in football is what happens on the field – and too many people are feeling sorry for themselves." In fairness the former chairman had a point. It was easy to accuse him of financial mismanagement and put the blame solely down to the way he ran the club. There were obviously two sides to every story. Yet ultimately, Ridsdale inherited a club in good financial shape and under his stewardship the club lost its healthy financial status and the chain of dominos perhaps could only have then been rescued by a billionaire investor with enough impetus to gut the club and start from scratch.

Gerald Krasner and his assorted investors paid £22.5m to secure ownership of Leeds United and they gradually reduced the club's debts from £103m to just over £30m. At one point Leeds were threatened by liquidation but continued stabilising enabled the club to keep trading. As a result the finances were stabilised but the team continued to underperform as less talented players were attracted to the club, mainly because Leeds could only afford to pay wages akin to their new peers, the likes of Southend and Wycombe Wanderers.

Speaking on Radio 4, Ridsdale was defiant regarding his running of the club. "I still don't regret taking the amount of debt on we did," he said puzzlingly, "but I regret spending the amount of money on footballers. We did buy too many and [with] the manager, every time he said he wanted a footballer, we said yes. We should have said no." Indeed, according to Ridsdale the problem had been that Leeds simply bought too many quality players. "We had too many players who felt they should have been in the team every week who couldn't get in the team because we'd got 24 international players. Looking back, I would do things differently. I would challenge the manager more, run things tighter."

Most brazenly, Ridsdale claimed on the programme that he would not have allowed the club to drop as far as they did if he had remained in control. He insisted the main reason he left was due to pressure from supporters and admitted that things had "gone wrong" at the end of his five-year tenure, but, he persisted, "it's gone far more wrong since I left than it did while I was there. I think the people who succeeded me haven't demonstrated they have done a better job than I did, and I think to be honest there was a certain amount of briefing against me in the press to deflect attention away from other people."

Again, perhaps, he may have had a point. In his book, *Football and Gangsters*, Graham Johnson reveals a highly bizarre plot that came into play just after Ridsdale left Leeds United. Johnson writes that defenders Michael Duberry and fellow top-wage earner Gary Kelly were both targeted by gangsters, eager to do the club's new owners a favour by spiking Duberry in a doping scam and breaking Kelly's legs. "The plots and schemes followed the £22 million takeover of Leeds by a Yorkshire-based consortium in March 2004," Johnson wrote, "after the financial problems which Leeds has suffered since the departure of former spendaholic chairman Peter Ridsdale."

Kevin Blackwell, who was assistant manager of Leeds as Ridsdale departed but later took over full-time, was his ever frank self when he revealed that the "actual figure" Leeds were in debt was £119 million, not £103m. Blackwell revealed:

> "An email came to my office and it told me, 'some players might get paid; some might not.' I tried to keep it from them for as long as possible, because it was embarrassing. Some of the players I'd brought here had asked me beforehand if we were financially sound. I'd told them we were but clearly I'd been misled."

Blackwell would also be misled as manager of Luton Town when he was, at one stage, driven to pay players out of his own wages when they were not being paid due to a lack of club funds.

In fairness to Peter Ridsdale, as Graham Johnson tells it there were as many questions and worrying trends after Ridsdale left than there were during his reign, but the cynical may suggest that Leeds were an easy target for the underworld precisely because of Peter Ridsdale's poor management of the club's finances. A club steeped in debt that should be raking in the profits and may get back to that status one day, is always going to be ripe for underworld meddling. Ultimately, those responsible for aiming to injure or damage players and their careers were not successful but it is perhaps a further indicator as to why Leeds find themselves still in the financial and footballing doldrums as of 2010.

Though he had often punctuated his time at Leeds with a peppering of dishonesty it was clear Ridsdale was pulling no punches now he had left the club. With a brazenness which carried a begrudging magnetism, Ridsdale authored a book revealing secrets about his time at the helm of Leeds United. The book revealed that Ridsdale placed a large part of the blame at the feet of his longest serving manager, David O'Leary (who let's not forget was the man who took Leeds so close to a Champions League final). Ridsdale even revealed that goalkeeper Paul Robinson stated, "I'll never play for that bastard again."

According to the former chairman, Robinson was not alone and O'Leary had lost the dressing room, with many players promising to move on if the Irishman was not relieved of his duties. Ridsdale also accused O'Leary of being directly involved in a secret deal with agent Rune Hauge over the transfer of Rio Ferdinand. The deal with Hauge cost Leeds an extra £1.75m, which was the agent's commission. Deals such as this had long been blamed on Ridsdale but he broke his silence and instead claimed he had proof that O'Leary brokered the deal. O'Leary responded by telling the *Daily Mail*, "I signed a confidentiality agreement, which was incorporated in a Premier League tribunal order, and so did Leeds. I have honoured that but I now feel compelled to defend myself against this deranged man." According to O'Leary he felt he had remained friends with Ridsdale – the former chairman even recommending O'Leary to Aston Villa chairman Doug Ellis for the manager's role at Villa Park – and was therefore baffled when the lid was apparently lifted on behind the scenes shenanigans at Elland Road.

It seemed Ridsdale may leave football altogether having parted from the club he supported, but it wasn't long before he headed a group who took on Barnsley, though this was a very short-lived association (although some claimed the club were heading towards liquidation under his tutelage) and instead Ridsdale returned to what he knew best, firstly becoming deputy chairman and, in October 2006, chairman, of Cardiff City. Following the same ethos he employed during his first years with Leeds, Ridsdale engaged the local Cardiff community, meeting and speaking with fans and offering his mobile phone number and private email address to all fans who were interested and resolved to answer any queries.

Yet just because a chairman presents himself as open to questions does not mean he will always answer them candidly. In fact, Ridsdale actively misled Cardiff fans over a season ticket initiative, known as the Golden Ticket Scheme, that he personally launched. Ridsdale denied that the scheme promised fans that advance season ticket sales would be used to buy new players, but this was stated in the club programme as well as on the official Cardiff City website. Therefore a £3m cash injection was received with fans happily laying down the cash. Unbeknownst to them, however, Ridsdale used the money to clear some of Cardiff's debts, including a portion of their £2.7 m debt to HM Revenues & Customs, and no new players were purchased.

Many fans protested at this news, some supporters holding up signs asking, "Where's my money gone?"

Ridsdale had openly said in the press that there was money to pay HMRC as well as Cardiff's other debts, insisting new players could be afforded with the season ticket income. He offered an extra incentive for fans, promising their money would be refunded if Cardiff won promotion to the Premier League in 2010. Ridsdale promised that this part of the agreement would be honoured despite there being no money for new players. When it was revealed no new players would be brought in, Ridsdale told the press:

> "I will eat humble pie. I say to our supporters, if I
> misled you – and clearly you feel I did – I apologise. We
> undoubtedly have some short term challenges and these
> challenges will be addressed fairly and squarely, and it
> would not have been appropriate to add to our overheads
> by bringing in players until they've been resolved."

Ridsdale was asked the inevitable question regarding his resignation but he was defiant, insisting he was staying at Ninian Park. Paul Abbandonato, a staunch Cardiff City fan of *Wales Online*, suggested:

> Whether he goes in one week, one month or one year,
> Peter Ridsdale must know deep down that his time as
> Cardiff City chairman is pretty much up. Once you get a
> situation where a 2,000-strong baying mob start calling
> for your head outside the ground, your immediate
> employment prospects look grim. In a way it's a shame,
> because Ridsdale has also done a lot of good things for
> Wales' biggest club.

The group of 2,000 fans made their protest before the game against Middlesbrough on 6 March, marching on a fifteen-minute walk to the stadium. More than 2,000 people also signed an online petition which was launched to convince Ridsdale to resign. According to an informed source I interviewed, Ridsdale is "loathed in this part of the world". He is also nicknamed "The Riddler" by many Cardiff fans.

Paul Abbandonato acknowledged that Ridsdale oversaw the securing of the new Cardiff City Stadium as well as being at the helm of a club which reached the FA Cup Final and has seen City make strides towards the Premier League. "Through some canny, poker-faced transfer dealing with other chairmen, he has netted remarkable sums of money for the likes of Michael Chopra, Glenn Loovens and Roger Johnson, amongst others," said Abbandonato, laughing that, "Heck, Ridsdale's the man who even persuaded someone at Plymouth to part with half a million for Steve MacLean!"

At the beginning of 2010 Peter Ridsdale apologised to Cardiff's supporters for the ongoing financial crisis at the club but insisted he would not resign and would stabilise the club's affairs. For the second time City were required to pay an outstanding tax bill, which stood at £2.7m. Failure to do this can result in administration. According to many reports, the club were on the precipice of liquidation.

Ridsdale, defiant as ever, made assurances that the club was "trading as normal" and there was "no immediate threat" to the future of the club. The most worrying word was perhaps "immediate". Was this a slip of the tongue? Is the fate of administration an inevitability for a club like Cardiff? It all sounds promising to invest in a new stadium and to make a giant leap forward in order to become a top division club, but the situation bares resounding similarity to the earlier scenario at Leeds. The prospect of high level success is always alluring to fans, especially those who haven't had much to cheer about through their club's history (the one and only time Cardiff finished as runners-up in the top division was 1923/24), but if it ultimately dictates that the club lives beyond its means then the resulting "success" is a contradiction in terms.

Though Cardiff can hardly be accused of harbouring a bevy of world-class players, their wage bill is still a quite astounding £1.2m per month. A Malaysian business deal had long been mooted to the Cardiff supporters, with Ridsdale travelling to the Far East before the 2009/10 season in the hope of securing additional investment to help City's ailing finances. Surprisingly, there was no magic deal or even a suggestion of investment from any of the wealthy businessmen Ridsdale wined and dined in Malaysia. However, property tycoon Dato Chan Tien Ghee became an additional director of the Cardiff board before the season began. There were also rumours that Tien Ghee would be the one to spark Cardiff's financial revival as he was purported to be investing £6m of his personal fortune into the club.

Cynically, many Cardiff fans aware of the situation felt Ridsdale would hang on as chairman in order to procure a portion of this investment for himself before leaving others to it. They were certainly right to be cynical of the amount rumoured to be invested and questioned whether this would serve much purpose, with the club still owing a minimum of £15m. This was a debt Ridsdale inherited, and was initially over £24 million, which he has since claimed to have been partly remunerated. The previous financial backers of Cardiff, Switzerland based investment company Langston, issued a statement which revealed they were initially willing to make a quiet repayment deal, but as Cardiff had repeatedly ignored their requests to discuss the debt they had to go public with a lawsuit.

Regarding Dato Chan Tien Ghee's appointment to the board, Ridsdale revealed, "The deal will almost certainly include sponsorship and we are already talking about shirt sponsor, stadium naming rights and an investment". The proposed deal would create a situation similar to that at Everton, with Asian sponsors that would bring in the huge and lucrative Far East market. Tien Ghee said:

> "I am very proud and privileged to be joining the board of Cardiff City at this time. Now that the infrastructure is in place, I believe that together with the existing board I can help to provide Cardiff City with the additional resources it requires to achieve the ambition of attaining Premier League Football and of making Cardiff City a recognised household name across the Asian continent."

"But I must stress you don't do things overnight," Ridsdale added, which is a sensible summation of a long-term investment process. At the same time it must be noted that Tien Ghee, christened "TG" by Ridsdale, is a billionaire whose business partner Vincent Tan ranks as one of the world's richest men. "Dato" is not part of Tien Ghee's name; it acts as a title, similar to a knight of the realm in Britain. Effectively, Chan Tien Ghee is Sir Chan Tien Ghee thanks to his services to Malaysia, such as a £500m pound Lido Boulevard Waterfront City project in Johor.

The idea of stadium naming rights references a particular area of criticism regarding Ridsdale's business dealings. According to my source, in the process of creating Cardiff City Stadium, Ridsdale allowed the "'fitting out' costs [to] run £7m over budget". The City chairman, who earns a £350,000 annual salary for running the club, "paid himself a £100,000 bonus which was agreed to be paid when the stadium was completed." My source also claims that on top of this, the club "owes a string of local businesses money", including one such business who were forced to add their name to HMRC's winding up order to illicit payment of a few thousand pounds from the club.

Like most managers, current Cardiff boss Dave Jones prefers to get on with his job of creating a decent team on the pitch and leave financial affairs to his chairman. But it is inevitable the manager will be involved at some point, even if it is as simple as the team's performance coming under inevitable scrutiny. Is Jones always going to be able to match the expectations of the bosses who pay his wages? When Cardiff lost 3-0 to Preston North End on 27 February 2010 there were apparently a few words exchanged between Jones and Ridsdale, a suggestion the manager later shrugged off. According to BBC reports, the heated discussion took place in Cardiff's dressing room in full view of the players. It was rumoured Ridsdale was unhappy with the team's performance and Jones rebutted with a complaint at the lack of fresh faces after he was forbidden from buying any new players in January.

Jones tried to change the emphasis in his post-match interview, focusing on the squad at his disposal, insisting "the players must knuckle down". Just three days before the match, Cardiff's second top scorer, Michael Chopra, was fined for being drunk and disorderly following a night out in Newcastle town centre, the city of his birth and the home of his former club. The 26-year-old was arrested along with an 18-year-old friend at 1.30am and spent a few hours in a cell before being issued with an £80 penalty. Though far less severe, the incident sparked comparisons with the behaviour of some of Ridsdale's former employees in Leeds. One cannot, of course, place any blame at the feet of the chairman for such anti-social behaviour, yet if Cardiff are to have aspirations to be a top Premier League side the slipshod attitude behind the scenes would have to cease.

Though some aspects of Ridsdale's recent career could be put down to bad luck or coincidence, there has to be an element of continuity in his perilous business deals that have now affected two major clubs. Though the existing debt of Cardiff City was no fault of Ridsdale's, and in this day and age no novelty at most clubs, it has to be said that, firstly, £30 million is an awful lot of debt for a club of Cardiff's size and, secondly, why, with his turbulent past at Leeds did Ridsdale get involved with a club who were not solvent? Isn't it just asking for trouble to take over an ailing club and purport to be bringing back the good times, preparing them for mass success which may or may not happen? Cardiff came extremely close to Premier League status at the end of the 2009/10 season, losing an intriguing encounter to Blackpool in the play-off final. It was indeed ironic that Blackpool, who ran a tight financial ship and carried less noteworthy players than the Bluebirds, managed to overturn the Ridsdale empire.

In hindsight, this might have been a good outcome for Cardiff.

In April 2009 Ridsdale's WH Sports went into liquidation after amassing debts of £410,000, £374,000 of which was owed to HM Customs and Revenue. According to the *News of the World*, "Cardiff's latest set of accounts showed WH Sports were paid £325,000 by the Championship club in 2008 for 'consultancy services'."

This paled in comparison to the £1m Ridsdale's firm – of which he and his wife Sophie were the two company directors – received from Cardiff the year before, when Cardiff's accounts showed they lost £5m. According to Ridsdale the £1m was "a bonus for saving the club from administration" and the chairman claimed he reinvested it in Cardiff shares.

Perhaps the greatest tragedy of Ridsdale's reign at both Leeds and Cardiff is the lack of accountability (pun intended) that the chairman had to face. Should any chairman be allowed to pay their own personal company a bonus when their main responsibility is in a mountain of debt? Does Ridsdale not receive a big enough salary in his day job? Is it really all about personal greed or is there a higher purpose at play here?

Unfortunately, despite the figures, which certainly do not lie, there are more questions than answers where Peter Ridsdale is concerned. Perhaps he should have been a politician. Perhaps he is one. The barefaced bravado and spinning of stories is a knack Ridsdale has in abundance and certainly a knack for spin that Alistair Campbell would be proud of. Even when the facts and figures say otherwise, Peter Ridsdale will smile, calmly explain the opposite and walk away unscathed. All the while, thousands of supporters oppose, furrow their brows and demand something be done. I'm not sure anything can be.

It seems Ridsdale is protected from up on high. In most walks of life a businessman who has done so much to bring a limited company to its knees would be paying that debt off for the rest of their life, or at least paying the price for a very long time, be it by a severe lack of opportunities or a ban from the business they once dealt in. To be allowed to walk into a club of a similar size to the one you plundered just a few years before seems preposterous. As we have seen with certain managers – accused and sometimes proved to have partaken in several distasteful practices – they can walk into the training ground the next day with the water on their back flowing into a nearby drain as they continue to disrupt, rather than further, their club. Where does the power truly lie?

Dato Chan Tien Ghee was announced as the new Cardiff City chairman prior to their play-off defeat, with Ridsdale stepping down and the Malaysian owning at least 30 per cent of the club. Cardiff City currently owe £15m which is due to be paid in full by 2016. By then Peter Ridsdale will be long gone, though one suspects his spectre may still loom large.

Sources: *United We Fall: Boardroom Truths About the Beautiful Game*, Peter Ridsdale (Macmillan, 2008), *Football And Gangsters*, Graham Johnson (Mainstream, 2007), BBC Radio 4, BBC Radio Five Live, *www.bbc.co.uk*, *The Sun, Daily Mail, Guardian, News of the World, Malaysian Sports*, Paul Stenning interviews,

WASTE OF MONEY!

4: MIKE ASHLEY AND THE DEATH OF NEWCASTLE UNITED

"To play for Newcastle and to score goals out there on St James' Park was a dream come true for me. You have to actually come from Newcastle to appreciate that."
– Alan Shearer

Newcastle United have a proud history; of that there is no doubt. It is also illuminating to compare the Newcastle eras of success and drudgery. Newcastle were founded in 1892 and, until 1997 when Sir John Hall bought the club, they were a private company owned by shareholders. When Hall, a property developer from Ashington in Northumberland, bought Newcastle in 1991, the ownership structure suddenly changed shape dramatically. Before Hall's involvement with the club, Newcastle were effectively run by the people, for the people.

For instance, their former chairmen included the likes of John Cameron and Joseph Bell. Cameron had been born in Perthshire but moved south to look for work and settled on Tyneside. His family were original shareholders in Newcastle United and so began a mutually respectful relationship, with Cameron acting as chairman from 1894 to 1895 and 1904 to 1908. Cameron was beloved by his players and associates at the club. When he died in 1916, leaving a widow and eight children, Cameron's true reverence was revealed. The club – directors, investors and players – raised a then substantial sum of £768 in order to assist the grieving family.

Joseph Bell was at the heart of United's great Edwardian set-up, acting as chair between 1908 and 1909 and earning the nickname "Uncle Joe". The Newcastle native would often lead the team out onto the pitch and was rarely away from his players. In this period there was no such thing as a manager so a chairman's influence was all important. Bell was an original director of the club and was responsible for the club moving to St James' Park.

There was a multitude of owners, chairmen and directors over the coming years but Newcastle remained firmly in the grasp of men who cared about the club and its development, whether they were local politicians eager to gain favour in the area, or long standing associates of Newcastle United. Usually those who were given the privilege of running the club were Tyneside natives. This tradition was upheld when Sir John Hall took over the club's affairs.

Hall may have ultimately sold Newcastle down the river but his overall impact cannot be underestimated. Touted as perhaps the most powerful man in the North East, Hall guided Newcastle – who were, in 1991, something of an ailing giant – from a modest single figure turnover to a highly successful business with a turnover approaching £50m.

In 1997 Hall floated Newcastle on the stock market and his stated aim was to see them turn into Newcastle Sporting Club, a supposedly bigger and better institution. However, the plan didn't quite work out as intended and it was Hall and his business partner Freddy Shepherd who ended up owning the majority of the shares in Newcastle United. Hall later stepped down, enlisting Shepherd to represent the club as chairman. The club was run this way until Mike Ashley took over in 2007.

On the pitch the Magpies had been successful, particularly at the beginning of the 20th century, as well as the 1920s and 1950s. They were winners of the top division in English football four times in the early 1900s and were frequent travellers to Wembley in the 1950s where they picked up the FA Cup no less than three times in four years – a glorious total made firm by the men of perhaps the greatest line-up in Newcastle team history. Their names stand as beacons of quality in the pantheon of Magpies legend: Jackie Milburn, George and Ted Robledo, Jimmy Scoular, Len White, Ronnie Simpson and future Toon manager, Joe Harvey.

Before Alan Shearer there was little argument who the greatest player to ever pull on a Newcastle shirt was – the Geordie legend Jackie Milburn, known affectionately in the North East as "Wor" (Our) Jackie. When Ashington's most famous son died in 1988, at the age of 64, the streets of Newcastle were lined with almost as many people who frequent St James' Park on a Saturday afternoon, such was the admiration for the man. He scored 177 goals in 353 games – even scoring six goals in one half at his trial for the club.

Milburn is the talisman of Newcastle history – successful history at that – but aside from his extraordinary goalscoring record, he was not unusual in his approach to the game. Milburn and his fellow professionals, all of whom were paid a pittance in comparison to today's footballers (even at the height of his fame with Newcastle Milburn was earning £17 a week), did not distinguish between his fame and his job on the pitch. For Milburn, Newcastle was a passion and he saw little difference between himself and the thousands who lined the terraces at the Leazes and Gallowgate ends of St James' Park every week. When Milburn arrived for his trial at the club he was wearing borrowed football boots and carrying his lunch – a pie and a bottle of pop.

Bobby Charlton would later say, "I walked through Newcastle with him many times. Everybody would say 'Hello, Jackie', and he knew half the names. He was a very well loved character in Newcastle."

Milburn's legacy does not exist just because of his phenomenal record and spirited performances for the Toon; he resides in local folklore because he was also of the same working-class calibre as the fans who paid to see their idol. Milburn had grown up in the coal-mining town of Ashington, where he worked as a heavy machinery fitter. Many Geordies worked similar jobs all the way up until pit closures during the 1980s and 1990s, and it was this working-class mentality which coloured Newcastle United's performances. They were often managed by hard men who didn't enter into softly spoken team talks or tactical nous – players performed out of a mixture of dedication, work ethic and fear of losing their jobs should they not perform well enough. Even the famous England manager Alf Ramsey was described by Milburn as being "like a good chicken farmer. If a hen doesn't lay, a good chicken farmer wrings its neck."

For the majority of their history, Newcastle United have maintained this work ethic and strong working class traditions. However, fans have always expected to see the addition of flair and attacking spirit on top of the basics. If it isn't hi-octane, guns blazing for 90 minutes there will be complaints. To take a modern example, after being relegated to the Championship for the 2009/10 season, leaving the Premier League for the first time in its history, Newcastle made a sterling start to the new campaign. Yet many Newcastle supporters voiced their displeasure at the style of play on the pitch and the turgid nature of 1-0 wins or scrappy 0-0 draws away from home. For Newcastle, winning is not enough, promotion is not enough; it has to be achieved with style.

With this in mind it was no surprise to find Kevin Keegan employed as manager in 1992. Keegan was a familiar face to anyone interested in football but for Liverpool and Newcastle fans he was also a playing legend (he scored 48 goals in 78 games for United). This attacking propensity held dear by Keegan saw his natural relations Newcastle United flourish under his stewardship. They managed promotion from the second division before eventually engaging in close battle with Manchester United for the 1995/96 league title, something which had not happened for seventy years. Only Sir Bobby Robson would emulate the required playing style and the requisite standard in the coming years, guiding Newcastle to two consecutive years of Champions League competition and thrilling crowds with attacking wing play and comeback glory.

Robson was perhaps the last hope for a club with such fierce standards and traditions – it seemed if he couldn't win a trophy as Newcastle manager it was perhaps unlikely to ever occur again. Even at the beginning of his tenure at Newcastle, Robson was in his late sixties and perfectly represented the old-school footballing–working-class tandem.

Yet this institution was dying out. The sober penchant for traditionalism and such obscene requirements as good sportsmanship and passion for your club had been savagely extricated from the modern game by the television and media globalists. Nowhere was this better represented than the sacking of a passionate, dedicated, working-class statesman born in County Durham. Robson lost his job because Newcastle were in the bottom half of the table, despite the fact it was only August and the 2004 season was just beginning.

In between Robson's tenancy and Kevin Keegan's dramatic return, the Toon featured three managers in four years – all of whom represented a disappointing succession of missed opportunities, lost points and lacklustre displays. It was just before the vacation of Sam Allardyce, who had presided over just 24 games as Newcastle boss, that Newcastle United found new ownership in the form of billionaire entrepreneur Mike Ashley.

Ashley became sole owner of the club in July 2007 after two months of negotiations whereby he purchased Sir John Hall and Freddy Shepherd's individual stakes in the club, ultimately becoming owner at a cost of £134m. However, Ashley later admitted he did not realise the scale of the club's debt, revealing there were outstanding payments to sponsors Northern Rock and outstanding liabilities on past transfers, which he was unaware of. One such anomaly, which was typical of previous contracts drawn up for players, was the ridiculous insertion into Damien Duff's contract that he was guaranteed £70,000 a week. There were no relegation clauses inserted into players contracts, which meant that when Newcastle were eventually relegated in 2008, Duff was entitled to the same weekly wage for the remaining two years of his contract. He therefore had to accept a wage cut to join Fulham and remain in the Premier League. But potentially Duff might have stayed. What did it matter to him if he was on £70,000 a week (thanks to Newcastle's recklessness), whether he put on a pair of football boots or cleaned his Range Rover?

Ashley also inherited the strikeless wonder Alan Smith who currently can claim over 70 appearances for the club without a single goal, despite his status as "attacking midfielder", one who managed 38 goals for Leeds United. It has to be said that for the most part, in recent years, Smith has been utilised more as a holding midfielder, yet he is still apt to play high up the pitch wherever possible. Smith's contract, overseen by Sam Allardyce, featured a welcome assertion for the Yorkshireman. Regardless of the division Newcastle played in, regardless of whether he even played, Alan Smith was entitled to a guaranteed £3m a year salary.

These relatively small mistakes added up to large debts for the Geordie giants, but it was a manageable shortage for a billionaire. The public were unaware of these financial anomalies, however, at least initially. For Newcastle fans it seemed too good to be true that they were receiving investment from a billionaire, one who did not shirk publicity in the way he once had. Before investing in Newcastle, Ashley was a vapour, even to the 8000 staff he employed around the United Kingdom. It was reported by the Guardian that only a single photo existed of Ashley, one from a junior squash tournament when he was a teenager.

Michael James Wallace Ashley was born in Burnham in 1963. The *Guardian* reported that Ashley's parents still live in the Buckinghamshire village in a "modest bungalow". Ashley attended Burnham Grammar School where deputy head Margaret Fleet remembers:

> "Most kids are fairly malleable. You can kind of subtly change their views about things. Mike was different. I remember him having quite strong views about things and being quite determined. It doesn't surprise me that he has gone on to be successful. I remember him talking to his friends about his Saturday job in a sportswear shop, and talking about how one day he would own the shop."

Upon leaving school aged 16 Ashley wasted no time in setting about his ambition. Rather than find a job he worked for himself, opening small sports shops in and around London. By the time he was 27 Ashley owned three shops which all carried the Sports Soccer name. Before 2000 he opened 100 more. Ashley also entered into the business of acquiring brands, particularly those which were largely considered to be in decline. Among the labels he took over were Donnay, Lonsdale, Everlast, Dunlop Slazenger and Karrimor – establishing a reputation for buying into golf, tennis and boxing brands. But Ashley's key business strategy was in also stocking leading sports brands such as Nike, Adidas and Reebok. He often made a loss on these items, pricing them way below the market average and drawing in shoppers who he reasoned would then pay for his own brands. It worked. In order to cut costs Ashley also resorted to using cheaper materials than had previously been used on once quality brands such as Lonsdale and Everlast. Often these products would not stand under scrutiny when washed or worn more than once. The company also often labelled garments as a size larger than their actual measurements.

Behind the scenes Ashley developed a reputation, even amongst his friends, as a reclusive, cagey penny pincher. As one friend told *The Sun*, "I remember laughing because he told us one day that he had traded in his Cavalier for an F reg Sierra. He did have a flash car – a BMW 7 series – but you would never see him driving it."

According to reports Ashley divides his time between two mansions in Hertfordshire and counts the Beckhams as nearby neighbours. His main home is a stunning 33-room mansion worth £25 million, which houses a private cinema, an indoor and outdoor pool complex and five garages.

Despite Ashley's lofty financial status he initially found favour with many Newcastle fans mainly due to his willingness to join them in local pubs and clubs for a pre-match pint, and also his insistence on wearing only a replica shirt in even the coldest weather (though it must be noted there is heating provided in the area where Ashley sits). Ashley also scored points when he received warning from Sunderland officials that he would not be able to wear a Newcastle shirt in the corporate box during the North East derby at the Stadium Of Light. Ashley's response was to join the fans in the away section of the ground.

Despite the fact that Ashley installed his friend, London lawyer Chris Mort, to act as chairman, he remained relatively popular amongst the fans. His biggest coup was to administer the return of Kevin Keegan to the club in January 2008. This fairytale reunion of "King Kev" with the club he so dearly loved should have carried a stark warning and in fact it was often acknowledged in the press that one should pay heed to the adage "never go back". In truth, many cynical United fans were rendered unimpressed by the installation of Keegan – the simple fact was that the Newcastle squad comprised many journeyman pros or those in the twilight of their career. Previous signings such as Mark Viduka, who had been acquired during Sam Allardyce's reign, were simply not of the calibre required to implant Newcastle back to the heights of the top four.

Ashley's hope was that Keegan would take care of the necessary business on the field while he struggled with the reality that Newcastle would not only have to dig deep to satisfy Keegan's priceless ambitions but also compensate those who were to leave in Keegan's wake. Sam Allardyce and the majority of his backroom staff were offloaded to make way for the new era of Newcastle success. Perhaps this was the time the past fifty years of hurt were to be banished. At the time, with his £1.9bn fortune burning a hole in his pockets, perhaps Mike Ashley considered the £5m he had to pay in compensation to his former employees a mere snip.

The expectation was that the enigmatic Keegan would be raiding the Magpies' funds on a regular basis to improve the relatively weak squad he inherited. Yet Keegan would only preside over two major signings for the club, paying £10.5m to Deportivo La Coruna for defender Fabricio Coloccini and an undisclosed fee for left-winger Jonas Gutierrez who had previously been linked with a £10m move to Portsmouth. The fact that both

Keegan's additions were South American was significant. On paper, buying two highly rated Argentinian international teammates was not debatable, especially when Gutierrez had a reputation for attractive attacking football. Behind the scenes, however, there was a power struggle developing. When Allardyce and co. departed the club, Newcastle had employed a number of replacement staff who included Dennis Wise – installed as director of football – and Tony Jimenez who was given the title vice president of player recruitment. Former apprentice footballer and non-league youth coach Jeff Vetere also joined the triumvirate as technical co-ordinator, which lent Newcastle a supposedly "continental style" management structure, according to the press.

Despite this restructuring there were early rumours of friction between Keegan and Ashley; the reluctance from Keegan to appear before the media in the build up to the new season was one indication that all was not well. The surprising addition of only three new players (the third was Danny Guthrie) and the persistent rumour that Ashley was looking to sell the club were all that was needed to fuel the fire. But when a smiling Keegan unveiled Coloccini and curbed the media gossip, the scandal appeared to be unfounded.

"We all understand our roles. We all understand what each other's briefs are and what each of us brings to the club and that is a good thing," Keegan said at the unveiling of Coloccini. Keegan was also quick to praise the Newcastle owner, insisting, "If you talk to Mike Ashley about this club, he is really committed. He would be the first to tell you he does not understand everything about football because he is a fan but I would guarantee what he does not know, he will learn very quickly."

Less than three weeks later, however, there was new speculation in the press concerning Keegan's despair at how the club was being handled. Dennis Wise was in honour of an influential position at Newcastle United where apparently his duties consisted of scouting for players, with Keegan given the final say as to whether a player was signed. Wise was an associate of Tony Jimenez who was a friend to both Mike Ashley and former Tottenham boss Juande Ramos. Keegan certainly knew of Jimenez's newfound influence at St James' Park as Jimenez – a London based millionaire property developer – was crucial in bringing Keegan back to Newcastle.

According to *The Times*, Keegan was aware at the beginning of his second spell at the club that the new model for Newcastle would include targeting youth players and then selling them on at an inflated profit. This would explain why so many young players from United's academy have risen through the ranks over the past few years since Mike Ashley has been in charge at the club. Nile Ranger, Andy Carroll, Calvin Zola, Ben Tozer and several more have all found a space on the Newcastle team sheet in recent times.

Jimenez, who was born in Brixton but comes from a Spanish family who hail from Seville, used his fluency in Spanish and knowledge of the city of Seville to help Tottenham hire Juande Ramos as manager, installing the Uruguayan Gus Poyet as Ramos's assistant in the process. Jimenez had established both Poyet and Dennis Wise as future contacts and friends while the two were Chelsea players.

In theory of course the structure at the new look Newcastle seemed sensible: recruit former players with a sound knowledge of the game, successful businessmen with notable industry contacts with a specific slant towards South American players (remember Newcastle's penchant for flair footballers), focus heavily on young talent brought in through the club's youth system, pin a Toon legend at the helm as manager to keep the fans happy and build from scratch. Unfortunately, the reality was only Ashley and his cohorts, from whom Keegan stood apart, were satisfied with the plan.

In reality it meant Kevin Keegan was going to be persuaded to bring in players who would be of no use to his plans as a football coach. Keegan was trying to build a team, an 11-man juggernaut, to bring back the passion and prestige to Tyneside. He wanted players who bled black and white whether they were born in Durham or Durban. Notoriously, it was Keegan's man management skills that suggested he would be the one to instil pride behind any football team. His own plan was to build 11 world-beaters and a squad of sturdy reserves, in much the same mould as those successful sides of the 1950s.

Yet those heady expectations were being tempered by Ashley's pursuit of quick profit. Towards the end of the January transfer window, Newcastle sold winger James Milner to Aston Villa for £12m, a move Keegan opposed. Milner was representative of the type of player Keegan sought to maintain Newcastle's reputation as a fast-paced, attacking side, and he was a player who had yet to reach his peak; in short, a player perfect for Keegan to mentor. There were also rumours of Michael Owen, Joey Barton and Alan

Smith leaving St James' Park, which appeared to anger Keegan given he seemed to have no say in whether they were sold or not. And when Keegan was approached about buying a player to garner favour with two agents for future prospective deals, Mike Ashley's house of cards suddenly began to look as shaky as the Magpies' defence.

By this time another Ashley associate, London businessman Derek Llambias, had joined the Newcastle ranks after Chris Mort quit as United chairman to return to his business interests. Llambias held a meeting with Dennis Wise and Kevin Keegan on 3 September 2008 to discuss Keegan's increasing frustration with issues behind the scenes. The rumours, this time, proved to be accurate – Kevin Keegan was extremely angry as he felt he wasn't being given the respect to run team affairs of his own accord. Keegan was seen leaving the meeting, claiming he had been sacked. It later emerged Keegan's second reign at the club had ended under the term "constructive dismissal".

An extract from the independent arbitration panel's verdict on Keegan's constructive dismissal revealed how the manager had felt his position was untenable given he had been forced to sign Ignacio González, a midfielder from Uruguay. The statement revealed:

> Mr Wise telephoned Mr Keegan and told him that he had a great player for the club to sign, namely Ignacio González, and that he should look him up. Mr Keegan tried to locate him on the Internet but could find no reference to him. Mr Wise told him that he had been on loan at Monaco but having checked out the details, Mr Keegan was unimpressed and told Mr Wise that he did not think the player was good enough.

Mr Wise then told him that the player was on YouTube and that Mr Keegan could look him up there, but he found that the clips were of poor quality and provided no proper basis for signing a player to a Premier League club. Moreover, no one at the club had ever seen him play. However, notwithstanding that he made it clear not only to Mr Wise but also to Mr Jimenez and to Mr Ashley that he very strongly objected to the signing of Mr González (he was to be signed on loan with an option to purchase), the club proceeded with the deal and the transfer was concluded the following day, on 31 August 2008.

The report concluded:

> The club did so because it was in the club's commercial interests to do so. The 'commercial interests', according to the club, were that the signing of the player on loan would be a 'favour' to two influential South American agents who would look favourably on the club in the future. The loan deal cost the club nearly £1m in wages for a player who was not expected to play for the first team but no payment was made by the club to the agents in respect of the deal.

The arbitration tribunal awarded Keegan some £2m in damages (plus interest accrued) to his salary and his reputation. But the reputation that suffered the most was that of Ashley, Wise and co. who were suddenly subjected to the scolding soubriquet of the "Cockney Mafia", a phrase coined by a banner-wielding Newcastle fan. Every single person in a position of authority at Newcastle came from London, which seemed somewhat incongruous to the history of the club.

Though Keegan hadn't exactly set the North East on fire since his return, fans were astute enough to realise it was going to take some time for Keegan to undo the mess left by his predecessors. They reacted angrily to the manner in which a talisman for Newcastle United had been treated. There were a number of protests against Ashley and the Newcastle board of directors, culminating in demonstrations in and outside the ground before, during and after a 2-1 home defeat to Hull.

Ashley responded with a wordy statement informing the media and the fans that he had put the club up for sale, insisting there was no need for further protests as he had "got the message". Ashley's statement was occasionally convincing but also seethed with a bitterness rooted in self-justification. "I hope the next owner is someone who can lavish the amount of money on the club that the fans want," Ashley sneered, perhaps aggrieved that the club had lost £60m in TV and sponsorship money after their relegation.

He continued:

> "I paid £134 million out of my own pocket for the club.
> I then poured another £110 million into the club not to
> pay off the debt but just to reduce it. The club is still in
> debt. Even worse than that, the club still owes millions
> of pounds in transfer fees. I shall be paying out many
> more millions over the coming year to pay for players
> bought by the club before I arrived."

Ashley was outwardly adamant he had done little to weaken Newcastle; on the contrary he had stabilised the club and lessened the debt, anchoring the bank balance. Interestingly he compared Newcastle as needing the kind of long-term plan of an Arsenal, indicating the Magpies would never be able to compete with the likes of Manchester United for spending power. This was intriguing given Malcolm Glazer, the owner of Manchester United, is valued at £2.2bn. Ashley, of course, is stated as having a worth of almost £2bn so there is little difference in terms of pure financial power. The question seems to be: how much of Ashley's substantial fortune was he willing to plough into a football club, one he had no particular affinity towards? This perhaps is the crux of the modern financial dilemma affecting football clubs. They are not run for the love of the club or in order to win trophies to please the fans, they are run in order to provide either amusement for wealthy businessmen or profit, every businessman's favourite word. It is a minor gamble for someone of Ashley's financial clout to risk £134m on a posh Subbuteo set. Before relegation to the Championship – and even despite this – the club would still have been worth a similar figure to Ashley's original investment.

When Ashley was panicking and attempting to offload Newcastle before they became an even bigger liability (he wasn't to know the team would make a tremendous start to the 2009/10 season) his price fell from an unrealistic £300m to an eventual loss on his original investment. Newcastle United were on the market for a mere £100m. It seemed to be less about their true worth and more about Ashley making a quick sale. "This will not be a fire sale, Newcastle is now in a much stronger position than it was in 2007," Ashley reasoned. "It is planning for the future and it is sustainable."

Yet if Ashley had reduced the club debts and had originally invested £134m then surely the club would be worth more than £100m?

Throughout August and September 2009, local businessman Barry Moat was reported to be in negotiations with Ashley over the sale of Newcastle. Moat would have made a popular choice with many Geordies; he was a local businessman and an associate of Alan Shearer. In fact newspapers were excited to learn Moat was chairman of Shearer's testimonial committee in 2006 and that the first thing he would do if in charge of the club would be install Shearer as manager on a permanent basis (Shearer had temporarily taken charge of team affairs towards the end of their inevitable relegation campaign in 2008).

Moat was a millionaire with diverse business interests across the North East, including significant property holdings and a development portfolio. Altogether he owned 13 North East based companies. He was also in possession of a luxury executive box at St James' Park and it was widely reported that he had invested in the club's youth academy several years earlier. A source close to Moat was quoted saying, "Barry is Newcastle's best hope of salvation. Talks are well advanced, although nothing is signed yet. He's a Newcastle fan through and through. He loves the club and has been devastated by what's happened. He'll do everything he can to make this deal happen."

Yet circumstances behind the scenes were rapidly descending into farce. It was continually reported that Mike Ashley was yet to be convinced Moat had the necessary funds to secure a takeover, yet for once Ashley was not the spoilsport. Rather, Moat's chances of success hinged on Barclays. The bank, who sponsor the Premier League at a cost of £30m a year and whose net income for 2008 totalled £5.287 bn, were dubious at the earning potential of Newcastle given their relegation to the Championship. In essence they sought a £10m payment as a convincer. Newcastle's previous overdraft had totalled £40m, but after relegation to the Championship the bank were about to withdraw the facility leaving Newcastle owing Barclays some £20m.

Without an interim payment of £10m plus interest, the bank refused any further lending. Moat could not afford the extra funds and was dependent on the quick sale of Newcastle's most valuable players. Yet the Magpies' squad was becoming further depleted after the loss of nine players and the compensation of just one on loan. Equally, those touted for sale, particularly Fabricio

Coloccini and Jonas Gutierrez, were going to be hard to sell at their required fees. Only Steven Taylor, the Geordie defender who played with passion and dedication, was worthy of his fee (a mooted £2m), though this was some way short of his true worth. Luckily for Newcastle, the supposed interest from Everton did not move on any further than a perfunctory inquiry.

Newcastle also had a problem with one of their biggest playing assets, Michael Owen. The England striker had been purchased for £16m from Real Madrid. Despite his dwindling reputation within the game, it was believed he could reignite his career playing for a top-flight English side. He couldn't. Owen just wasn't producing the goods at Newcastle. Instead of his usual average of more than a goal every two games, on Tyneside Owen was barely scoring a goal every three. To add insult to injury (and he was frequently injured) Owen could have left the club before his contract ran out but declared his loyalty to Newcastle, only to leave as soon as his contract was up – meaning the club lost out on a potential transfer fee. Instead, the £16m that had lured Owen from Madrid dissipated into the negative equity pile while one of football's richest individuals joined Manchester United.

Things got worse for Mike Ashley in September of 2009. His company Sports Direct was allegedly £400m in debt and he had also lost tens of millions on bad business deals, and Ashley was hit with the insult of a fraud investigation when JJB Sports finally got their revenge on the Newcastle owner. In 2005 Ashley blew the whistle on JJB for fixing Manchester United and England shirt prices at an unreasonable £39.99. After an investigation JJB were fined £6.3m. They returned the favour four years later and Ashley's corporate headquarters in Derbyshire were raided under investigation for price fixing and fraud. The *Guardian* reported that, "If the OFT finds competition law has been broken, Sports Direct could face a fine of up £140m." As for the fraud aspect of the investigation, it was revealed that, "Offences such as failing to disclose information also carry penalties of an unlimited fine and up to 10 years in jail."

Despite Ashley's financial struggles and despite the fact they were represented by a caretaker manager in Chris Hughton, Newcastle made a tremendous start to the new season. After two months, with the club sitting on top of the Championship, Mike Ashley decided to stick with his investment (perhaps he also wanted to hold onto one of his biggest assets in case of a huge fine from the SFO) and on 27 October 2009 the club were withdrawn from sale. Business-wise this was most likely a shrewd move, but for the supporters of the club the dark days were destined to continue.

As if to rub salt in the wound his tenure had caused, Mike Ashley dealt a hammer blow to all locals who had grown up with their local team's ground being St James' Park. The oldest and largest stadium in the North East had been Newcastle's home since they were formed and had always been known as St James' Park. But in an all too familiar scenario in the modern era, Ashley announced the club was to sell naming rights to the club's stadium at the behest of clearing their mounting debts. On 4 November 2009, it was announced that Ashley's own company would sponsor the stadium, rebranding it "sportsdirect.com@St James' Park Stadium" until the end of the season.

BBC Radio 5 live football commentator John Murray, himself a North East native, represented many fans' attitude when he remarked

> "Many of Newcastle's supporters will be sceptical and also disgruntled that Mike Ashley's ownership of – and relationship with – the club is set to continue. And however much stadium naming rights are part of football in the 21st century, let's see how many of them refer to St James' Park as anything other than that once a sponsor's brand is nailed onto it."

Perhaps one of the most worrying aspects of the blatant disregard in renaming traditional sites and stadiums may be the potential renaming of parts of the ground which are named sentimentally. In 1988 when their ground was being extended Newcastle proudly opened a new West Stand at St James' Park and named it after Jackie Milburn. In the future could we see the great Jackie Milburn's name tainted, when, in a fit of greed, an owner decides the earning potential of a stand name is more important than the legacy which the original name represents?

In Newcastle there are two statues of Jackie Milburn, one of which stands at Milburn Junction, just a few steps away from St James' Park. The statue, which, unlike many, bears a fitting resemblance to its subject, stands as not only a mark of respect to a beloved Geordie icon, but also to the last era of true success Newcastle United enjoyed. It is a bitter irony that the group of men, who often still worked their regular job whilst representing their club, were so successful at the highest level.

Today, Newcastle United pays out almost a million pounds in wages every week to its staff – a figure which would have bought the entire back catalogue of United players from 1892 to 1955 (the year they last won a major trophy). Newcastle fans of every generation would happily trade their millionaire representatives who perform often perfunctorily on the pitch for a glimpse of the type of silverware once held aloft by men like Jimmy Scoular – a man who served in the Royal Navy during the war before joining Newcastle – who was acknowledged as being "as tough as they come".

Despite the fact Newcastle actually managed to return to the Premier League after just one season away – thanks to the heroics performed by rookie manager Chris Hughton – the club is still wracked with controversy courtesy of Mike Ashley who will no doubt be pleased he has hung on as owner, seeing his stock inevitably rise with promotion. Yet in just two years Mike Ashley has bestowed Newcastle United with relegation, five managers and record financial losses. But perhaps the greatest tragedy is not the amount of money wasted, but that Ashley and his ilk will never know the pride men like Jackie Milburn and Alan Shearer felt when representing the legend that is Newcastle United.

Sources: *The Sun, Daily Mirror, Guardian, Paul Stenning interviews, BBC, Wikipedia, Observer, The Times, News Of The World, Financial Times, Newcastle Chronicle, www.nufc.com.*

5: ROMAN ABRAMOVICH
FOOTBALL'S REVOLUTIONARY COMMISSAR

"Wealth is empowering. Wealth can uplift communities from poverty. A white man gets wealthy; he builds Wal-Marts and makes other white people money. Wealth is passed down from generation to generation. You can't get rid of wealth. Rich is some shit you can lose with a crazy summer and a drug habit." – Chris Rock

Mention the idea of wasting money in football terms and it's inevitable Roman Abramovich will be mentioned. The Russian former toy salesman has revolutionised the Premier League with his vast wealth and no fear attitude. He cares not for sentiment or tradition within the game, perhaps because he doesn't understand it. Abramovich has, more than any other owner in the history of football, looked upon his club as a business and profit making opportunity.

There is little truly known about the man and that which has been made public smacks of a PR coup designed to humanise a man who is essentially a machine-like money maker.

The story goes that Roman Arkadyevich Abramovich was an orphan by the age of four and was raised by a makeshift Jewish family close to the Arctic Circle.

There is nothing else known of Abramovich's childhood – the biography always jumps to his business beginnings which, according to all and sundry, included selling plastic toy ducks from a Moscow apartment. Mention this and an image appears in the mind which features a full bath of water and a scant offering of rubber duckies which poverty stricken Muscovites could come and view in order to buy cheap presents for their children. The reality – if it is to be believed – was a little more advanced. The Russian, who was born on 24 October 1966, was manufacturing plastic ducks and sailors after a few small business successes which included selling black market goods such as deodorants and perfumes. Abramovich apparently tripled a £1,000 investment which had originally been a wedding gift from his wife's parents.

As a young man Abramovich served as a private solider in the Soviet Army and it was during this period that he began his urge to trade and make profit. It seems incomprehensible that a soldier had the time and inclination to score business deals whilst serving under a notably harsh regime, but this is certainly confirmed by those who knew "Roma" at the time. Nikolai Panteleimonov, a former army friend of Abramovich says, "The two of us hit it off immediately. We served in a rocket force unit stationed in the town of Kirzhach – a small town in the Vladimir Oblast."

Panteleimonov explains that the future oligarch showed commendable and unusual enterprise even at the age of 20. He explained:

> "Roma was head and shoulders above the rest when it comes to entrepreneurship. He could make money out of thin air. A soldier's monthly allowance was 7 rubles back then. It's not enough if you have a sweet tooth or a date you want to take to the movies during leave. Roma came up with a scheme. Roma was selling the stolen gas to the officers of our unit, charging them 20 kopeks a litre, instead of 40. And his customers knew well where that fuel was coming from. But they didn't report the case to anybody. Every party involved was quite happy: the officers could buy gas for their cars at half price while the soldiers could pocket some extra money for their own needs. Abramovich kept a part of the profits for himself. He also bought ice cream or pastry for his helpers – a sort of incentive for the work well-done."

Abramovich ended up "helping out" his superiors on a variety of issues. It was clear that he would go far. However, none of his fellow servicemen could foresee that he would become one of the richest men in the world.

He purportedly made his fortune from a series of oil-export deals in the early 1990s. Along with Boris Berezovsky, Abramovich took over oil giant Sibneft at a fraction of its true market value. By 2000, when Berezovsky fled Russia whilst being pursued on fraud charges, Abramovich became sole owner of the company. But in 2005, he sold his 72.6 per cent stake to Gazprom (the sponsors of CSKA Moscow) for around $13bn.

In 2003, the ubiquitous football agent Pini Zahavi helped bring Abramovich to Chelsea. He had been introduced to the Russian two years earlier in Moscow by a mutual friend and he furthered their friendship by inviting the billionaire to a Champions League match between Manchester United and Real Madrid in April 2003, two months before Abramovich would buy Chelsea. Zahavi was critical to the deal being finalised and was complimentary and positive about his friend and the contribution he would make at Stamford Bridge. "What was Chelsea before Roman came?" he asked the *Observer*, rhetorically. "It was two days before going bankrupt. The situation was a disaster. The chief executive at the time, Trevor Birch, came and he really begged. 'Help me,' he said. 'We cannot pay the salaries.' Now, Chelsea are one of the best teams in the world. And that's because of Roman Abramovich's money."

Zahavi was instrumental in the introduction of Avram Grant to Chelsea, who would would take over managerial duties from Jose Mourinho after first becoming director of football. Grant had previously been manager for both Maccabi Tel Aviv and Maccabi Haifa where he was good friends with Zahavi. The agent would also broker the deal that would take Grant to Portsmouth when the club were struggling in late 2009.

As with other current Premier League club owners, Abramovich has not given freely to Chelsea, but rather indebted them to his philanthropy. Chelsea's 2007/08 accounts show Abramovich was owed £488m by the club though by December 2009 the club released a statement revealing that this had been converted to equity. It was boasted that the club was virtually debt free. Abramovich of course would be the benefactor of such a deal and the ownership of more shares suggests that there is either a massive sale on the horizon, or Chelsea expect to be winning a European trophy very soon.

In 2007/08 Chelsea had a £190m turnover, but their 'operating profit' was a figure of minus £11.4m. Their overall net debt came in at well over half a billion pounds with a regular monthly interest payment of £700,000. Since

Abramovich installed himself as Chelsea chief, the club has won numerous competitions and have only been bettered by Manchester United in their quest for trophies. The one competition which has eluded them so far has been the Champions League and it seems Chelsea will do anything to win it. But the competition, much like our own FA Cup, is not as predictable as it once was. If the tournament was only about money then Chelsea would be victors every season. There are plenty of backbiters in football who clearly resent the multi-billionaire status of 'Chelski'.

In November 2006 Chelsea came under renewed attack from Karl-Heinz Rummenigge when the Bayern Munich chairman complained that Abramovich's funding has distorted competition in European football. According to Rummenigge there was no hope of clubs outside the big television markets of England, Spain and Italy making their mark in the Champions League. Rummenigge was clearly envious of the continuing loss forfeited by Chelsea, which is consistently mopped up by the club's illustrious owner. Speaking in the German football magazine, *Kicker*, Rummenigge complained, "I doubt whether in the next 10 years there will be a German club in the final of a European competition. Given what Abramovich does every summer in the transfer market, how can German clubs stay competitive?"

Yet it was a resounding surprise, especially perhaps to the Bayern chairman, that his club indeed reached the 2010 Champions League Final where they played, ironically, Jose Mourinho's Inter Milan.

With great money and power indeed comes great responsibility, but Roman Abramovich is perhaps the only modern billionaire owner who has managed to retain that responsibility with any degree of convincing grace. Unlike many of his peers Abramovich has not only been a success at a club who were floundering, he has shown he is in it for the long haul. Even if it only means ten years – or whenever Chelsea win the Champions League – Abramovich will truly have revolutionised the club and, in turn, the game itself.

Given he has shown he is willing to absorb huge spending sprees, it is perhaps more amusing than galling to read about Abramovich's exploits. Certainly his personal choice of who to revitalise Chelsea as manager at the time of his takeover was a remarkably shrewd move. It is hard to see that Abramovich picked Jose Mourinho merely for his success at FC Porto (though a manager who had won the Champions League with a team of unfancied domestic players put him in good stead for the trophy Abramovich most craves with Chelsea). Steve McClaren has proved to be a success in the Dutch league with FC Twente after a widely touted disaster spell in charge of England. Winning a league over the two heavily established favourites in Ajax and PSV Eindhoven (not to mention Feyenoord and AZ Alkmaar) is certainly a great achievement, but would McClaren have had the necessary charm and cunning to rule the English media the way Jose Mourinho managed in every season at Stamford Bridge? In employing Mourinho Abramovich showed great decision making abilities as well as an impressive awareness of the nature of football in England.

Chelsea's overall debt in 2010 is almost £750m, which would be cause for concern to most owners. Roman Abramovich, though, is not most owners, and seems capable of bucking the trend where the slightest financial indiscretion means avoiding the questions and making a quick getaway. With Chelsea not exactly being dominant on the continent, the proposed plan to make the club a world beater seems to be taking much longer than one might have anticipated. Still, Abramovich is showing patience and currently, at least, absorbing the losses at the club himself. This, therefore, is surely not a sign of weakness at Chelsea, but rather a signal of their strength. With an owner willing to take defeats on the chin and financial turmoil in his stride, there is perhaps less of a question mark over Chelsea than any other club mentioned in these pages.

Nevertheless the profligacy of Abramovich does deserve special attention. For a publicity-shy, somewhat reclusive figure, he certainly manages to have his wealth examined in the most minute of details without fear of continuing to spend lavishly.

Abramovich had previously enjoyed a solid marriage with his second wife Irina – with whom he has five children – but in October 2006 the couple announced they were to split, with Irina hiring two of the best divorce lawyers in the UK. This was reportedly because Roman had been enjoying a "close relationship" with Dasha Zhukova, the former girlfriend of Russian tennis player Marat Safin. Zhukova was born into wealth as the daughter of Russian, London-based oil magnate Alexander Zhukov. The *News of the World* reported at the time that the potential divorce settlement was likely to be the highest of all time, at a proposed £5.5bn. However, Roman and Irina later divorced in Chukotka (where Abramovich was at one stage governor) in March 2007, with Irina receiving a figure believed to be in the region of £200m.

According to Russian business daily, *Vedomosti*, the figure includes the value of homes in Britain and in the Moscow region, as well as a yacht and private plane. Abramovich can certainly afford it. In 2009 he started building work on a £150m house situated behind Harrods department store. This is to be the most expensive residence in the United Kingdom. The planned development, over five storeys above ground and three basement levels, includes a cinema/entertainment room, an indoor pool, steam room and sauna, as well as a children's study and entertainment room. All six family bedrooms have en suite bathrooms, as do the two guest rooms. In a linked mews development behind the main building, four flats above a multi-car garage are to be used as servant accommodation. Abramovich had carefully purchased the entire building step by step, buying individual flats – he himself has long lived in one of the flats in the Lowndes Square district – until he eventually owned the whole building.

Abramovich's unique spending sprees are the stuff of legend and may have little to do with football, but show the almost reckless, careless mentality of the Chelsea owner. He does what he wants, when he wants and doesn't care what anyone thinks or says. For example, Abramovich was in Baku, the capital of Azerbaijan, and felt an urge for sushi, which the country did not seem to cater for. Abramovich's aide ordered £1200 worth of raw fish from Ubon in Canary Wharf, which was driven to Luton airport, then flown by private jet to Azerbaijan. The estimated cost? A mere £40,000, which for a takeaway lunch, is some going. But, as pointed out in the pages of *Money Week*, the mere logistics of this kind of process suggest there may be an element of exaggeration to such stories. Even in a relatively obscure country there must be top eateries to a person of Abramovich's distinction, and even if there were not, half a day to wait for your lunch is a long time by any standards. The conclusion is either these kinds of stories are untrue, or at least exaggerated, or obscenely rich individuals such as Abramovich take part in this kind of over indulgence simply because they can.

When spotted eating at Nello's restaurant (a favourite haunt of stars such as Jay Z) in New York, a member of staff somehow leaked a copy of the receipt for Abramovich's table. It showed the Russian spent $47,221 on lunch, which included two bottles of $10k champagne and a tip of

$7,328. Abramovich flaunts his staggering wealth with little shame. He has several yachts the most extravagant of which features a military-grade missile defence system to keep the oligarch safe. His Eclipse yacht is also equipped with armour plating surrounding the bridge and Abramovich's master suite, as well as bullet proof windows. There's also a submarine that can be launched underwater and dive to a depth of 160 ft that doubles as an escape pod, as well as two helicopter pads.

Abramovich is also involved in art, a pastime Dasha Zhukova is also apt to dabble in. The Russian holds the record for the biggest price paid for a post-war work of art, after he purchased Francis Bacon's Triptych for around £55m, and he also paid a record (for a living artist) when he purchased Lucian Freud's Benefits Supervisor Sleeping – a fairly grotesque depiction of a fat woman on a couch.

Despite his wealth dropping to an estimated £7bn in the 2009 financial year, Roman Abramovich still occupied a place on the *Sunday Times* Rich List, which placed him as the 39th richest individual in the world. This made him wealthier than the Duke of Wesminster, the Nike owner Philip Knight and even the Italian prime minister Silvio Berlusconi. Only Lakshmi Mittal superseded Abramovich in terms of wealth in the UK.

So, with all this ridiculous wealth, why should Chelsea still be in debt? Would their accounts read anything close to Portsmouth? In fact it is very likely, the only difference would be the potential income, or indeed, that the losses can be offset at the flick of a switch at a Swiss bank. For the club to have creditors to the tune of £736m (most of which comes from Abramovich himself of course) shows remarkably bad running of a club which should not only be operating at a regular profit, but should be more than capable of paying its customers and whoever else is involved at Stamford Bridge. Much like Portsmouth's succession of billionaire owners, Chelsea are in a position for one man to clear the club's debts instantly and return them to solvency. Realistically, what is the point of paying extortionate prices and wages for players, agents and managers when success is only ever fleeting and brings little by way of financial recompense? Football has certainly become about money for the most part, but when that money is only ever enjoyed by those at the very top, what is the incentive for the rest of those involved with Chelsea FC?

Abramovich is an extremely shrewd, intelligent man. He is not crazy enough to continually put his own money on the line in order to pay those players, agents and managers. It may seem that way but if he is effectively indebting the club to his services, then he is merely loaning "his" club a small portion of his own capital, capital he surely expects to be returned to him as and when he leaves the club. The income provided to Chelsea by Abramovich is not a donation; it's an interest free loan. Essentially he is having fun – hoping for glory in the interim – but risking very little in terms of his actual wealth. Ultimately it will only be the club that suffers. If Abramovich sold to a less canny investor, and after Portsmouth's dire run of investors anything is possible, then Chelsea could easily find themselves in administration quickly. Chelsea's chairman, Bruce Buck, has stressed that Abramovich "loves football" and will not "walk away" from Chelsea.

Yet Chelsea's accounts make for perilous reading. They show that, were Abramovich to tire of running their club, he would want the entire amount of his investment returned, and Chelsea would have just 18 months to find the money. Undoubtedly this would then be dependent on a new owner with as much in the bank as Abramovich. It would certainly require a billionaire to continue to fund Chelsea in the style which they have been accustomed. Should their designs on a global brand fail then Abramovich may well lose interest; at present he seems to be aiming for long-term success but considering he can do whatever he likes, when he likes, Chelsea are being run on an everyday tight rope.

For all their success, for all the fans they picked up with the charm of Mourinho, for all their attractive football, the club is still nowhere near the heights set long ago by the likes of Manchester United and Liverpool. They possibly will never reach those heights. Money does not make an institution. If this were possible then Major League Soccer would have taken off a long time ago. No, tradition and long-term success come from within, not without. Sir Alex Ferguson has been in large part the one responsible for Manchester United's modern success, but it has taken him and the club as a whole 25 years to reach the heights they currently occupy. Is Roman Abramovich willing to put another 15 years of his life and his money into Chelsea at the behest of one day mimicking United's impressive business model?

Should football owners really be able to hold a club to ransom in this way? They are not owners if their investment is due back to them, they are merely lending their money to a club at the behest of success which, if it doesn't materialise, means they will want that money back. If this is acceptable then why should fans absorb losses out of their own pockets? Should fans not be able to have their investments returned to them if the club is not successful?

Why can't season ticket money be refunded, or the money spent on merchandise? Any owner would find this ridiculous, so why should we accept that an owner can receive his money back and place the club into unmanageable debt, with a position that can never be recovered?

So far, Abramovich has outstayed all newcomers to the Premier League, and to football as a whole, something which is to his eternal credit. Yet he is no different to other modern football club owners in that he wants to see an immediate return on his investment. To this end, even the highly successful managers have been offloaded; managers who would have been at other clubs for decades. What is it exactly that Abramovich wants? In football, as in many American sports where percentages count and are regularly used in a team's statistics for each season, a winning percentage of any description is something to be cherished. Anything between 55 and 60 per cent is considered gold dust to most owners, in whichever sport. Over 65 per cent is stupendous. Winning the Premier League, the FA Cup, the League Cup and Community Shield is obviously not enough for the Russian. There has to be a European return on his roubles in order to maximise the Chelsea brand. And then the European honours must continue.

Part of the reason Chelsea have not managed to create a global brand as of yet is that they lack European pedigree, in fact even domestically the team were distinctly unsuccessful in the pre-Abramovich era. Indeed the club might not have come into existence at all were it not for Fulham, who rejected an offer to rent Stamford Bridge in 1904. A Mr H. A. Mears must take credit for establishing Chelsea FC as he was determined to turn Stamford Bridge into a football stadium, rather than the proposed development by the Great Western Railway. Mears was convinced by Frederick Parker of the financial benefits of developing a major sporting venue. Chelsea was then founded. In their entire history, dating back to 1905, the club has won the top division in English football only once, in 1954/55, long before the Russian revolution took place at the Bridge. They had won the FA Cup three times before Abramovich and the League Cup twice, but this was hardly enough to establish them much further afield than West London.

In Europe the club have merely the Cup Winners' Cup to speak of, which they have won twice, in 1971 and 1998. That same year they also won the fairly meaningless Uefa Super Cup. In fact it may well have been the era of Gianluca Vialli – arguably Chelsea's second greatest manager of all time (after Mourinho, who might pip him based on the fact he won the league twice where Vialli did not) – that initially interested Abramovich. Vialli brought a style and substance to Chelsea which propelled them from a team who had, not long before, been a second division outfit. The Italian flair brought Chelsea much success, and it seemed having a European footballer, with Champions League honours to his name on board was enough to give the club a degree of awareness for the major European competitions. But despite this timely experience, even Jose Mourinho could not do better than bring Chelsea to one European final, where they would lose the Champions League to Manchester United, in 2008.

It is indeed with players and managers that Chelsea have wasted the most money. And given this is the main source of both their business and their revenue it will continue to be this way, most probably it will worsen. For less than eight months' work, Luiz Felipe Scolari was paid £16 million. His basic yearly salary was £6m, while his compensation pay off was £12.6m. This was small fry compared with the £18m paid to Jose Mourinho, though at least he was at Chelsea for more than three years and won a significant amount for the club. Altogether, Abramovich has paid £40m in compensation to the various managers he has moved on during his tenure. Scolari, perhaps, was an arguable case for the sack, having 'only' won 56 per cent of his 36 games in charge. Mourinho has a record of 67 percent (over a much longer period as well), and even Avram Grant was towing a miraculous 66.67 per cent despite having no experience managing in the Premier League. Grant, however, perhaps due to his lack of pedigree or flamboyancy, was relieved of his duties and he and his backroom staff were given a combined £2m payoff.

Chelsea chief executive Ron Gourlay has said Chelsea are still striving to eventually break even. "We are reducing our costs by controlling expenses, including salaries and wages," he claims. Chelsea, however, still have the Premier League's biggest wage bill. It is not so much their top players who are draining the club's resources – Manchester United, Manchester City and Liverpool all pay their best players similar figures – for Chelsea it is as much about the squad players being paid more than the Premier League average. Still, paying John Terry, Frank Lampard and Michael Ballack a combined total of £18.6m a year will dent the bank balance of any club. It is arguable that Wayne Rooney should be worth more in wages than John Terry at this stage of his career, yet even Rooney, who scored 26 goals in the Premier League in 2010, earns £5.2m a year, in comparison with the £6.5m paid to Terry.

Chelsea have not spent greatly in the transfer market in more years, yet their expenditure is still overwhelming. Their turnover has reduced from £213.1m to £206.4m. Net capital expenditure has reduced from £85.1m to just £4.2m following the completion of projects such as their Cobham training ground. Cash outflow has been dramatically reduced from £107.4m to £16.9m.

They have, however, occasionally been shrewd in the transfer market. They more than doubled their investment on attacking winger Arjen Robben while also profiting from decent free transfer signings. There is also the bizarre story of Brazilian defender Alex, who initially cost Chelsea £5m in 2004. Because Alex was besieged with work permit problems he had to be loaned to PSV, with Chelsea having the option to buy him at any point in the future for the princely sum of one dollar. Three years later they did just that.

Abramovich's time at Chelsea has certainly produced memorable players who have been of great service to the club. Names such as Didier Drogba, Ricardo Carvalho and Petr Cech spring to mind. Yet there are also countless bad deals, which of course are down to the manager rather than the owner. However, it is Abramovich who has bank rolled the purchases of certain big name flops and ultimately it is Chelsea who are going to be left responsible for their lack of success and drain on funds.

Since 2003 when Abramovich became Chelsea owner he has spent almost half a billion on transfer fees alone. The purchases, suggested mainly by Jose Mourinho, have for the most part been strong additions to an initially frail squad. Yet there has also been little by way of profit; recouping those fees through the sales of other players has never been Abramovich's strong point. And when he himself has become involved in the direct business of buying players the results have been disastrous. Take Andriy Shevchenko who was yanked from quite a happy position in Italy with AC Milan to be thrown together with a manager (Mourinho) who did not want him as a player. The upshot was Mourinho fell out with Abramovich and Shevchenko became Chelsea's biggest financial loss, scoring just nine goals at a cost of £3.4 million each.

Other purchases have been less costly but equally questionable. Asier del Horno was recruited as a left-back, despite Chelsea having Wayne Bridge, and cost the club £8m. He was sold to Valencia just a year later for £5m, having failed to settle in the Premiership. Seven million was spent on Geremi, from Real Madrid, another player who failed to find stability at the Bridge and who ultimately left for free after four seasons with Chelsea. The perennial runner (with little by way of finished product) Damien Duff was bought in a fairly ridiculous deal worth £17m but left Chelsea for just £5m three years later. He, like Geremi, ended up at Newcastle United. Another winger, Shaun Wright-Phillips, perhaps heralded greater promise and a bigger justification for a £21m transfer fee, but even he failed to live up to his potential, being sold on by Felipe Scolari at another loss of £12m.

Despite his complete failure at Manchester United, Juan Sebastian Veron was purchased for £15m but left on a free transfer when he was just as disappointing for Chelsea. Hernan Crespo would also leave for free in the end, despite being bought in 2003 as one of the world's best strikers and costing £16.8 million.

And then, of course, there is Adrian Mutu.

Pini Zahavi was a big reason why many of the world's major players were content to play for Chelsea and as far as Abramovich was concerned, he had been a vital person to befriend. Yet Zahavi was certainly rewarded for his helpfulness. In the first summer of Abramovich's reign, Chelsea spent £111m on new players, for which Zahavi earned a £5m personal cut.

The saga of Roman Abramovich is now inextricably linked to Chelsea; it has been their making but it may also be their undoing. As long as the Russian remains at the club they will be taken care of. The quote that prefaces this chapter should remind you of that. Anyone involved with oil is not going to have much of a problem in terms of financing, regardless of the markets or any financial crisis. But personal choice is another matter. As soon as Roman walks out of Stamford Bridge, the whole dream may just turn out to have been a shocking nightmare.

Sources: *Kicker, Independent, Vedomosti, Observer, News of the World, Guardian, Daily Telegraph, The Sun, Sunday Times, Money Week,* BBC, *Londongrad: From Russia with Cash; The Inside Story of the Oligarchs,* Mark Hollingsworth and Stewart Lansley (Fourth Estate, 2009), *Paul Stenning interview*

6: THE AGE OF BRANDING

"The Premier club in the Premier League – that is Manchester United!" – Martin Tyler

Manchester United. Manchester United. Manchester United. The brand name rings loud and proud and cannot be underestimated. Listen to a Martin Tyler commentary during any Manchester United match and you will be bombarded with the incessant chanting of the brand name that is Manchester United. Tyler will not refer to them as United, the Red Devils or any other derivative which may seem appropriate. They are always Manchester United.

The reason for this may be somewhat subconscious or it may be coldly calculated. Whatever the truth there are two absolutes:

1) Let's say Manchester United are playing Liverpool in a Premier League encounter and both teams occupy the top two places in the division, with the match being played at Anfield. By rights the commentator should mention both teams an equal amount of times during the 90 minutes. It's a little like possession – over the protracted minutes it will generally even out between two evenly matched sides. Yet Tyler will mention Manchester United, on average, three times as often as their opponents, even when those opponents are also of championship winning calibre.

2) Let's say Manchester United are playing Newcastle United. Manchester United will always be referred to

by Tyler as Manchester United, and Newcastle United –
for that is their full title – will almost always be referred
to (when they actually are named) as Newcastle.

Given point number two – which incidentally you can feel free to test during
any one of Tyler's Manchester United commentaries – one cannot make the
argument that Tyler, who is certainly a well spoken, erudite football man, is
merely attempting to give the club its due by referring to them with their
full title. If he does not do it for other teams then why should Manchester
United receive special billing?

The answer is important and can only fall into two categories:

1) The full billing is a subconscious twitch that may be
used simply out of admiration for the club, or perhaps
because Martin Tyler is reputedly a fan.

2) The relentless usage of their full title is a deliberate
advertising spin for which Tyler is somehow rewarded.
The Premier League is televised everywhere, from
Kuwait to Singapore. It is particularly popular in Asia
where Manchester United are the leading football
brand. Is this really a coincidence? I don't believe it is any
more a coincidence than the fact Tyler is almost always
the commentator for United matches and, incidentally,
always seems to be distraught if the side concede a goal.
Once again, listen for yourself if you don't believe me.

A brand is perhaps the most important part of a football club's desire to make
their club a profitable business. There is no secret to the importance of a brand
in the modern business age. Manchester United is a brand name, just as Gordon
Ramsay is. With a brand, a company can attach certain expectations of their
product. As far as United goes the expectation might be fast, free flowing football,
the Munich air disaster, Sir Alex Ferguson, George Best and Wayne Rooney.
Their history, tradition and actions are all wrapped up in the brand.

As far as foreign fans are concerned, there is no "United" as there is in the
working men's clubs of Stretford, for there is no local knowledge, awareness or

home grown passion. Can a fan in Malaysia feel the same desire for Manchester United to win as a fan born and bred within a few feet of Old Trafford? Absolutely, but the local connection can never exist and it is this home town team link to football which has characterised the majority of the history of the game. Traditionally, and outside of the top Premier League teams, this is still the case; supporters were tied to their local club for better or for worse and weren't capable of glory hunting – it usually isn't an option. Chances are, if your family are all Tranmere Rovers supporters, you will be too. Even if you deviate and take to supporting Everton there will always be a link with Tranmere.

With Manchester United now being a global business, the need to constantly reassert their dominance and brand is almost obsessive. They have now become a machine which is on a par with the ever present brands and products that adorn magazines, billboards and television on a daily basis. Look around in every day life – regardless of where you live – and there will always be adverts for Visa, Coca Cola, McDonalds Sony and Ford. Do we really need to be told about a can of Coke in order to buy one? Do we need to be reminded of Visa when we think of applying for a credit card? Probably not, but the adverts remain and cost millions for the companies to administer. The reason for this is that constant awareness of these major brands means you tend not to think of Dr Pepper when asked to name a soft drink, though ironically Coca Cola manufacture Dr Pepper in Europe anyway; dominance is also key to establishing good brand ethics.

The element of branding is imperative for even the biggest companies because it not only promotes their product incessantly, it also drives out the competitors who cannot afford the cost of major advertising. So it is with Manchester United. Regardless of who owns the club, whether it be a small time billionaire or one of Forbes's proportions, the brand name remains as popular as ever and cannot be destroyed.

There are only two things which could damage the brand of Manchester United:

1) A sudden lack of success on the pitch. No trophies and a finish of 17th in the Premier League for a few years would have a catastrophic effect on the club.

2) The removal of their brand from global football. This would of course happen if for instance they failed to

qualify for the Champions League for a few consecutive years, but it would also occur if they were not so heavily promoted in the media.

It is the relentless marketing which keeps Manchester United at the top worldwide.

Many people are convinced that teams such as United remain at the top because they have the best players and the most money but, as we will see throughout the course of this book, if it were about money then Queens Park Rangers would top the Premier League.

The brand of Manchester United protects them from the apathy many players might feel towards a club such as QPR. If Didier Drogba was offered £100,000 a week by Manchester United and £300,000 by QPR he wouldn't move to Loftus Road. Why? Because it's not just about salary. A player is lured in by sponsorship, privileges and the furthering of their own brand. Doubtless Drogba would further his career simply by playing at Old Trafford whereas he would have to work harder and play alongside ten other world beaters to achieve this with QPR.

It is this globalism to which all new investors and "big" clubs aspire. Just look at the strides Chelsea have made to become a global brand, with particular deference to Asia. This is no coincidence. And this is why it is so difficult for a club such as QPR to compete and further their own brand. Firstly, their history is not as appealing as Manchester United's and secondly they don't have Sky in their corner.

A very cynical (is there any other kind?) Liverpool fan has often argued with me that the only reason Manchester United are so revered is because of the Munich air disaster. He maintains that Liverpool are the more successful club overall but that because of Manchester United's "name" (read "brand") they will always be the top dogs. While it is, in my opinion, hogwash to attribute United's legacy to a terrible catastrophe, they have been lucky to survive with their brand name intact. During the late 1970s and early 1980s for instance they were not particularly successful, yet by the time of the revitalised side, under Ron Atkinson, the club recaptured its spirit and with it, its global reputation.

It is often the case that fans of leading clubs will debate over whose club is bigger or have ridiculous discussions about who was better, George Best or Kenny Dalglish? The aforementioned Liverpudlian believes the latter while anyone outside of L1 would surely concede it was Best. In actual fact these debates amongst fans of the bigger clubs usually concern seniority as opposed to true size. As far as branding goes, Liverpool aren't far behind Manchester United and they have their own legacy to protect – indeed their success in Europe has been the instigator to their worldwide recognition.

Liverpool have also exercised an important part of corporatisation and branding – a catchphrase. "You'll Never Walk Alone" doubles as a song from the musical *Carousel* and is an integral phrase with which Liverpool fans assign their identity. Few football fans are not aware of the Reds' tradition of singing this song before Liverpool games. The phrase is etched into the club crest and also adorns both the Shankly gate entrance to Anfield and the tunnel which leads onto the home pitch. Traditionally those players who feel a special affinity with the club will touch the crest before heading out to the turf.

Manchester United have their own catchphrase, "Pride of the North", which adorns certain merchandise, particularly scarves, though this is far less identifiable with the club and generally has more relevance for those who live close to the ground – after all if you live in Kuala Lumpur you won't be too concerned with bragging rights over Manchester City. It is a familiar criticism of United in modern times that their fans by and large do not live in Manchester. Scan the faces of many fans, especially in the sideline seats at games, and they are like a who's who of nationalities, often just as concerned with photographing a player on their mobile phone as actually watching the match or cheering on the team. And truthfully, many Mancunians have been pushed out by ticketing hell at Old Trafford with matches being expensive and very few spare tickets available to locals.

Yet from a business perspective, this suits United just fine. Though their headquarters are situated in a less than salubrious part of Manchester, way out of the main city centre (unlike rivals City), the club has managed to retain an air of glamour and superiority which is as much to do with their brand as anything else. Fans come from all walks of life and parts of the world to pay homage to the club and indulge in one of the most lucrative forms of profit for any club – the vast range of club merchandise.

In fact United's achievement in essentially disassociating their name and reputation from their actual location is a unique one, and something which sets them apart from their rivals. Aside from the Manchester music scene, in recent times there has been little to globally promote Manchester as anything other than a typical English city. In fact it has struggled, despite huge investment, to compete with the recognised glamour of London and will perhaps forever play second fiddle to the capital. But one thing Manchester does have is Manchester United; ironically it is not the mention of Manchester itself which instils love into football fans worldwide, it is the full brand of Manchester United.

The United marketing machine has been exceedingly clever (or lucky depending on how you view it) in targeting areas outside of its immediate radius and succeeding in developing a non-specific target audience; you don't need anything to support Manchester United other than money.

A look at the merchandising phenomenon is, as you would suspect, dominated by the top clubs, though in recent years other much smaller clubs have followed suit. Alloa Athletic who play in the Scottish Seconddivision command a following of around 250 regular match goers in comparison with Manchester United's 74,814 devotees, but the Wasps, as they are also known, have still entered into the realms of club merchandise. The club crest adorns everything from pencil cases to rain jackets, despite only being available in person at the club shop and strictly with payment by cash only. A mail order service is available but is only as reliable as the Alloa weather.

Visit the Manchester United superstore or their online club shop, however, and the range is simply enormous. Bathroom tiles, serviettes, confectionary, toys, games, car accessories – the list is endless. A Manchester United personalised dressing room photo will set you back a mere £29.99, while a personalised dressing room mug (a cup with your name on it) is a snip at £11.99. A bathtime plastic duck, of which Roman Abramovich may be envious, will cost a bargain £5.99.

It may be considered a waste of money by many to buy anything simply because it has the United club crest on it, but for the club it is an ever rolling torrent of profit. They manufacture a product cheaply abroad – ironically, often in Asia – and then whack the club crest on it and sell it at an often obscene profit. These incomings represent a huge proportion of overall club profit, as it does for many clubs in this materialistic age.

Of course, as with any brand or label, you are paying for the name. A plastic duck can be bought for 99p at most market stalls in Britain, yet colour it red and put a club badge on the side and it goes up six times in value. United's brand is a safe, reliable accompaniment to any product, and there is very little risk in producing anything that bears the name. Other clubs and investors have bent over backwards in order to procure this exact same reliability but a brand does not earn a distinction such as Manchester United's overnight.

If the club name is a brand and even the players are recognised assets and brands in their own right, then the club stadium must hold a special place as part of each club's branding policy. And so it has been proven. Ironically three of the biggest teams in the country have evolved into global brands by retaining the identity of their home ground. Old Trafford, Stamford Bridge and Anfield all speak of history, tradition and charm. The Emirates stadium remains the exception out of the top four and it was a sad loss to the game when Highbury lost its title.

The naming of a stadium in accordance with a company is perhaps one of the most ludicrous developments in the modern game, not only because of the tradition is lost with a name change, but through the bizarre suggestion that a football ground named after a company will, in turn, increase revenue for that company as it is essentially on permanent advertisement.

In the NFL in the USA, where football means something altogether different, this phenomenon has been in existence a little longer. It is not uncommon for a team to play in a stadium whose title bears no relation to the team or the sport. Some of the more preposterous include Indianapolis Colts' Lucas Oil Stadium and Pittsburgh Steelers' Heinz Field. Both teams originally held grounds with traditional names and meanings but commerce has usurped this practice. The habit has crossed the water and started to infiltrate the Premier League, worryingly it has also descended to the lower leagues. Even small clubs are eager to get their hands on any sponsorship or advertising revenue that they can. York City, for instance, signed a deal with Nestle to rename their ground Kitkat Crescent, though they still face potential administration. And here is the more worrying trend, that clubs are inevitably going to go underground while in the meantime they support and advertise a company which will only ever go into liquidation through choice.

But even in the big leagues, can a company seriously say that by a football ground being named after their brand, their sales will increase? It is as superfluous as shirt sponsorship and once again, will usually feature companies that can afford the ubiquitous advertising costs. Relatively smaller firms, however, will eventually be pushed out of the running. When considering shirt sponsors it is intriguing to think of the big teams who once proudly portrayed company names such as Sharp and Crown Paints. In time, these British institutions have been edged out of the market by global conglomerates and it is this incessant need for ever more loot which has sparked ground name changes. Perhaps it really is only a matter of time before Old Trafford is renamed as The Barclays Theatre of Dreams.

Barclays, in fact, represent the ultimate in superfluous spending. Currently sponsors of the Premier League, the bank spends a whopping £30m a year in order to hold the naming rights over the league. In addition to the title, they also receive advertising hoardings at Premier league grounds and a decorative ribbon bearing their title which hangs limply off the Premier League trophy. Though it seems unnecessary, to say the least, the company can afford it, as they carry a total worth of over £47bn.

Barclays were one of the first banks to become involved with the Premier League but in its time of sponsoring the competition there have certainly been many new banks entering the fold and sponsoring teams, competitions and stadiums – again a trend which first started in the United States. Yet it is Asia which truly carries the weight of footballing financial expectations and the two are inextricably linked. Take the Barclays Premier League Asia trophy which is a decidedly meaningless competition, designed merely to spread the name of Manchester United et al even deeper into Asia, wrapped up with the Barclays logo and furthering that minimal effort and investment long-term. This is not something that is seen as underhand or cagey, the sponsors openly admit their ultimate goals.

Bob Diamond, Barclays President, said at the time of Barclays' confirmation as ongoing Premier League sponsors in 2006:

> "I see the sponsorship of the world's best football league as a major strategic investment. We all know about the fantastic appeal of the Barclays Premiership in the UK but this sponsorship also fits our international presence and aspirations particularly in Asia and continental Europe. It provides us with powerful brand visibility in the many markets around the world in which we operate."

Deals with Asia are rapidly expanding and increasing. And it is Manchester United and Chelsea who are at the helm of the expansion to the Far East. Partially, both clubs are also brokering deals in America to increase the profile of their clubs on both continents. Control America and Asia and financially at least, you are controlling the majority of the world's potential revenue.

Take Manchester United's relatively recent shirt sponsors AIG (American International Group). The company is inherently North American, its headquarters based in New York City, but interestingly they were formed in Shanghai, China in 1919. Today they still have an Asian headquarters, based in Hong Kong. Ironically the company's founder Cornelius Vander Starr was the first westerner in Shanghai to sell insurance to the Chinese, a link he has with Manchester United who can certainly be considered one of the first English football teams to establish links with Asia.

AIG's involvement with Manchester United can certainly be questioned in terms of cost effectiveness. How can an American insurance company benefit from sponsoring an English football team when it is costing them £14.1m a year for a four-year period? In fact this deal was touted as the most valuable sponsorship deal in the world. Valuable is perhaps a word which should be changed to wasteful. Despite the fact United have won the Champions League and Premier League during the time AIG adorned their shirts, surely there can have been little financial reward gained by the company in having their logo slapped across replica shirts?

The American market for football is still as slow as ever, with Americans tending to prefer to play the game and create a positive environment for kids, instead of watching it on television. There was a further link to the AIG deal, however, which was that as part of their sponsorship deal, the insurance giant would oversee MU Finance, a revolutionary arm to the Manchester United beast that offered "services" for all United supporters. These services include the United credit card, savings, mortgages and, yes, insurance. Once again we return to the idea of a brand. One reason major companies continue to be successful is their trusted brand name. We may not enjoy the dominance of the likes of Visa and Mastercard but many of us have one of their credit cards because it is a trusted brand and you know what you are going to get. The furthering of the Manchester United brand over the past few years has enabled them to earn supporters' trust to the extent that they are now – on a worldwide basis – willing to part with even more of their money, lining United's and in this instance AIG's pockets even further.

AIG ended its sponsorship agreement with United in early 2009, though their logo was used up until the end of the 2009/10 season. Taking over the mantle were another American insurance company, the Aon Corporation. Indeed, with so much American investment it suggests the real reason the Glazer family became involved with United was to further their own links with multi-national American corporations, for that is truly where the money is. As if to underline this, the new deal with Aon is worth a reported £80m spread over four years, a quite staggering amount which again has less to do with shirt adornments and more to do with extracting a few pounds from each credit card purchase a Man Utd cardholder provides, or the commission from a United themed mortgage. It is not about having a mortgage through Manchester United of course, United are just the brand glue that holds your attention and trust. The real beneficiary will be the company running the financial services United sponsor. So, in a clever twist of advertising magic, Manchester United is really sponsoring Aon.

Despite United's American links, they are always furthering their Asian investment. In March 2010 the club signed an agreement with Telekom Malaysia, which according to the official website was, "to become its 'Integrated Telecommunications Partner' for the next five years. The agreement will also bring increased online content to United supporters and TM customers."

The company has the monopoly on Malaysia's fixed line network so it is similar to British Telecom sponsoring United. Upon signing the deal, United's chief executive David Gill commented that the club hoped the deal would increase United's profile in southeast Asia. "Anyone who went on our tour of the Far East last summer knows the strength of feeling that Malaysians have for the club," Gill said. "Over 40,000 attended our training session and another 40,000 came to the second match in Kuala Lumpur, despite only having 48 hours' notice of the fixture."

Gill is most certainly aware that United have their own monopoly. In a country that has almost fifty million inhabitants, one in four is a Manchester United fan. That is true branding success. Only by a limited "open field for one" where preference is given, can such a success happen – coupled of course with ever impressive performances to boost the trophy cabinet.

United are unique, but other clubs are attempting to follow.

Even where it seems as if another club has got there first, United were linked to a company first. In 2008 it was announced that Chelsea were joining the elite ranks of Hollywood's finest when the club signed with the entertainment's most powerful talent agency, Creative Artists. The company already represents Steven Spielberg, Brad Pitt and Tom Cruise. It also has a sports arm which was responsible for overseeing David Beckham's move to LA Galaxy and currently counts Cristiano Ronaldo as a client.

CAA Sports confirmed they would be involved with Chelsea in the areas of corporate partnership development, stadium development, athlete marketing, branding, touring, and corporate social responsibility. The usual fair-weather splurge was issued with then Chelsea chief executive Peter Kenyon saying:

> "Chelsea is delighted to be partnering with CAA Sports. CAA has unparalleled experience across a whole variety of areas that appeals to Chelsea. Together we can build on Chelsea's global business reputation, its unique position as the only soccer club in the centre of London, our talent, and our desire to be seen also as a force for good in our local community and around the world."

CAA said that Chelsea's international make-up – with a squad that features 23 national team players from 14 different countries – gave the "brand" a "global appeal". Peter Kenyon was so intrigued by the lure of Hollywood that he joined the company himself. With divergences such as this we can surely expect to see more by way of personal branding and club branding that aims to boost clubs' profiles in America and, doubtless, Asia. One thing is for certain, whether it be Sony, Ford or Telekom Malaysia, branding will not go away and looks certain to remain forever a part of our beautiful game.

Sources: *ICM News, Forbes, Wikipedia, Sport Business, Guardian, MU Finance, Sky News.*

7: HIT AND HOOP: THE STRANGE TALE OF QPR

"I didn't even look at the accounts or what other debts were owed, I only realised how much financial trouble we were in a little further down the line. But we just couldn't let that happen to this club. We were extremely close to the line at times." – Gianni Paladini

Queens Park Rangers, better known as QPR, may not have trophies bursting out of their Loftus Road cabinets, but they are still a popular club with a memorable history and tradition. Whether it be their unique blue and white hooped shirts or their once unique ownership of a plastic pitch, QPR are a prominent English football club. Yet the fact does remain that they have only ever won the Secondand Third division titles as well as the League Cup in 1967. In 1975/76 they were runners up in the top English division and they also came close to winning the FA Cup in 1982, but sadly for Hoops fans the history of QPR reads like a tale of the also-rans.

The club is one of the oldest in Britain, having been formed in 1885 (there is some doubt about the exact year – some suggest it was as early as 1882, others consider it to have been 1886) by the old boys of Droop Street Board School. When first formed the club were known as St Judes as the boys were members of the St. Judes Institute. However, most of the players came from the Queens Park district in London and so, when the club merged with Christchurch Rangers in 1886, the name changed to Queens Park Rangers. The man responsible for the club's formation was George Wodehouse, whose family maintained a connection with the club for the next hundred years. In fact, when the Wodehouse family cut their ties with Rangers it marked the beginning of their recently chequered financial goings on.

Initially QPR played in light and dark blue halves and the only equipment the club owned at the end of the 1880s were four posts and two lengths of tape for the cross bar. Still, they managed to play London rivals Tottenham and Fulham in friendly matches during the early part of their footballing life. The club struggled financially in their early days, in fact they moved to St Quintin's Avenue in 1901 as rent was cheaper, which was no surprise given the players changed into their kit in a local pub. Just a year later, however, after complaints from locals who thought the club were lowering the tone of the area, QPR moved back to Kensal Rise.

One of the team's most famous characters is former player and highly successful manager Alec Stock, who took the club to consecutive promotions from the third to the first division, during a period where he developed a good relationship with Rangers' famous chairman Jim Gregory. It was down to Stock and Gregory that QPR began to make a name for themselves; winning the League Cup as a then third division team did plenty to enhance their reputation and fondness with football fans. QPR are perhaps as well known for their famous players as their achievements and it's no wonder given they have fielded the likes of Rodney Marsh, Stan Bowles, Gerry Francis and John Hollins. The latter trio were part of the QPR side who ran Liverpool close to the League title in 1976, consequently seeing QPR qualify for Europe.

During the 1980/81 season Terry Venables was appointed manager and a year later QPR became the first League club to replace grass with an artificial playing surface. It was during this season that Rangers reached the FA Cup Final where they lost to another of Venables's former clubs, Tottenham. Venables brought a modicum of stability to Loftus Road, taking QPR to the first division and then a fifth-placed finish during their next season back at the top. Due to his success with the club, Venables left to join Barcelona in 1984.

QPR managed another 12 years in the top flight before they were finally relegated into the second division. Since then they have struggled for consistency but plans were afoot to bring them back to prominence in England and fight for a much vaunted top level trophy. In May 1996, media tycoon and lifelong Rangers fan Chris Wright bought QPR and instantly announced his Rugby Union club Wasps would ground share at Loftus Road. Wright was founder of Chrysalis Records, which he formed in 1967.

The record label became home to the likes of Blondie and Jethro Tull before it was sold to Thorn EMI in 1991. Wright later floated the newly formed Loftus Road plc, incorporating both QPR and Wasps, on the Alternative Investment Market.

However, Wright's plans were perhaps a little too lofty. Banking on QPR's previous spell as a top flight club, Wright reasoned that this was where the club belonged and where they must surely stay. Despite numerous big football names such as Ray Harford and Gerry Francis, as well as a very respectable spell in charge for Ian Holloway, who won 100 of his 252 games in charge, QPR could not break out of the second tear. In just over ten years the club washed £35m down the drain due to excessive running costs and an over ambitious outlook which banked on the club remaining in the top division throughout the 1990s and securing the increasing television revenue being given to Premiership clubs. Of course, they did not expect to be relegated, or to struggle to climb back to the top division. Wright lost over £10m of his own money. A lot of Rangers's expenditure went on players who ultimately did not produce a return on Wright's investment.

In 1996, then manager Stewart Houston smashed the club's previous transfer record when John Spencer joined QPR from Chelsea for £2.35m. There was also £2.1m splurged on the hapless Mike Sheron, who, in fairness, had a decent record for Stoke City but just could not replicate the same form in London. The problem for QPR was clearly that they were spending above their means and banking on performances which never seemed to materialise. Rather than consolidate the club and stabilise their position in the lower tier of English football, Wright was convinced they would, at some point soon, qualify for promotion to the Premiership, at which point they would be besieged by income from television rights and new sponsorship and investment. Many clubs have gained promotion to the Premiership and put all their eggs in one basket – attempting to keep the Premier money rolling in and not countering with the "what if" scenario of relegation, such as Hull City in 2010 – but at least those teams got there first. It is one thing to over budget when there is at least significant income being generated. If that income is not even there and you are merely intending to reach those levels one day soon, that must be considered thoughtless and naïve.

By 2001, Chris Wright realised he had made a tremendous mistake and withdrew his investment from the club, prompting them to enter administration. Wright sought a buyer for the club but it appeared no one was willing to risk buying a continually underachieving club who were haemorrhaging money left and right. A statement on the club's website, referencing administration, read: "The decision has not been taken lightly and is a direct result of the losses incurred by the Group, currently running at £570,000 per month, over a sustained period of time." The holding club for QPR, Wright's Loftus Road group which included Wasps, admitted it had run out of money and its share listing was cancelled.

At the time there were rumours that former director of the club and property investor Andrew Ellis had offered £9m to buy QPR, promising to move them to a new west London site near Heathrow Airport, while redeveloping the existing ground. Wasps, meanwhile, had no trouble attracting a new buyer and they remained solvent. Just a month later, QPR fans tried to storm the directors' box where Wright was sitting, after Rangers lost to Fulham. Though Wright escaped unhurt, the incident was unsavoury enough to see him step down as chairman. From this point on Chris Wright was still involved with QPR but it was well and truly behind the scenes. The club continued under administration. Minutes from an official meeting in 2004 highlight the club's then ongoing difficulty in obtaining a buyer. Chief executive David Davies explained, "There has been no movement with any of the interested parties since November, but the Maurice Fitzgerald consortium were trying to meet with Chris Wright upon his return from Australia. The club is also looking at other things to try and take us out of administration."

According to Davies, the onset of administration brought QPR crashing "back to reality". Davies suggested, "Football is living in cloud cuckoo land and we are having to work on the cash we generate." He admitted at the time that the club's debts "currently stand at £6.7m to Chris Wright and £3.3m to other creditors."

During this time, Rangers were unarguably a club for the people, though it begged questions of morality, or lack thereof. Defender Danny Shittu signed for QPR in 2002 having been on loan initially. It was Rangers's take on third party ownership, with QPR fans Matthew and Alex Winton having a large stake in Shittu's role at the club. The Winton brothers paid £250,000 of their own money to bring the defender to Loftus Road, and they also paid Shittu's wages for his first season. Compared to some players,

Shittu was a worthy investment, performing well for the Hoops and going on to make 172 appearances.

The good will did not benefit the Wintons or the club, however. After also contributing to the costs for striker Aziana Ebele Mbombo, better known as Doudou, Alex Winton insisted:

> "We committed ourselves to sponsoring Doudou and Dan Shittu's £250,000 transfer fee from Charlton, which we did. Wages that were agreed with the club were to be met by We Are QPR, a fund we set up and to which fans were encouraged to contribute. It didn't take off as we hoped, but at no point did we suggest to the club that we personally were liable ... When you're a small club in Division Two, you have to get the fans to help. I believe over 50 per cent of clubs in the lower leagues will have funds set up like this in the next 10 years."

On 27 May 2002 QPR were taken out of administration, after a hearing at the High Court. Chris Wright still retained ownership of the club's training ground as well as a 25 per cent stake in the club as a whole. David Davies said, "This is wonderful news and the conclusion of one of the darkest periods in our history. We have faced some tough decisions and learned some hard lessons. We will come out of this experience in a much stronger position." Davies paid tribute to the club's supporters, who had seen their club wracked by player departures, forced in order to absorb club debts. This on top of administration did not dampen the fans' enthusiasm and in fact attendances were up, on average, at Loftus Road. The figures behind the scenes still remained surprisingly sketchy, however, despite the club being lifted out of administration.

It was indeed no wonder that David Davies had long been championing the idea of ground sharing as a means of extra revenue. Not only was there the potential of Wasps sharing Loftus Road once more – after they left for High Wycombe in 2002 – but there was also the "loan" of their ground to Fulham while the Cottagers home ground was being redeveloped. In fact it was this enforced time away from Loftus Road that left Wasps feeling no need to return to ground share.

The ownership of Loftus Road seemed to be under a veil of secrecy, with even the power brokers at QPR not quite sure who had the final say. Essentially the club were loaned £10m from the value of their ground, but they had to monitor Companies House and Land Registry records to find who exactly could lay claim to ownership of the land upon which the ground stands. After being confused with the suggestion that a Swiss trust owned the land, the club soon learned that it was in fact owned by the ABC Corporation. This is not the ABC television network in America, although it could be, as there is next to no information available on the ABC Corporation, though they were the same company that rescued Derby County with a £15m loan.

The only information revealed about the company is that their headquarters are in Panama, a tax haven which the Panamanian consulate proudly declares treats their clients with the utmost confidentiality. The confusion with a Swiss trust is understandable as it appears ABC is led by three Swiss lawyers: Peter Lenz, Marcel Muff and Hans Hinderling, who is a registered footballers' agent. But football finance writer David Conn later revealed when writing in the *Independent* that the former manager of Nissan UK, Michael Hunt, was the man behind the ABC Corporation. Previous rumours had suggested that Mohammed Al Fayed was the man behind Rangers's loan. Hunt had been convicted of conspiring to cheat the Inland Revenue in 1993, after Southwark Crown Court heard that Hunt, along with the company chairman and a director, had orchestrated a "truly massive" tax fraud which amounted to almost £100m. Hunt was said to have personally made £30m from the frauds. Ultimately it was inferred that the majority of the cash behind ABC came from Hunt, who operated a family trust in Switzerland that was worth some £100m.

The company were also making a million pounds a year just from charging interest to QPR for their loan of £10m. It is pertinent to note that the club would struggle to make a profit of £1m a year, thus leading to the inevitable question: how exactly can the club sustain that payment without entering even greater debt? It was the fans who initially suffered the cost of the interest payment to ABC, when season ticket prices increased by 50 per cent in order to generate some extra income. Future chairman Gianni Paladini later suggested he wanted to cut the interest payment in half. Paladini also alluded to a question most fans felt was important. "People must think there is some kind of mafia involvement here, but I want the best for QPR and I'm putting together the right people to achieve this," Paladini said. "The moment I came here I felt an affinity for the club, its fans and its history, and I wanted to get involved. I want to be part of the team that takes QPR back to the Premier League."

QPR fan Bill Power, who occupied a place as chairman on the Rangers board, criticised Hunt's involvement, saying "It is scandalous that we've been saddled with this debt, from a Panama corporation of all places, at such an outrageous interest rate." The scandal did not end with Hunt, however. Philip Englefield was thrust onto the QPR board in order to represent ABC's interests after they had loaned the club the £10m. Englefield's position was "consultant legal advisor", yet it was discovered by the QPR supporters trust that Englefield had been found to have taken £900,000 from one of his firm's client's bank accounts (in 91 separate withdrawals, for payments "of a personal nature"), and had been struck off the roll of solicitors by the Law Society. Englefield had also been convicted of theft and fraud for siphoning £4.7m from his firm's clients account. In March 1993 he was sentenced to seven years in prison, though he only served three.

After this information was made public, the club officially asked Englefield to step down, though he retained his consultancy role. Englefield is currently registered as a director of several property companies which are based in Knightsbridge. Harrods of course is situated in Knightsbridge – could this be a coincidence? It would be easy to link the source of funding to Mohammed Al Fayed, given he is the owner of Fulham FC who were ground sharing with QPR at the time, and the Knightsbridge connection instantly makes one think of Harrods, which Al Fayed owns. It would be hard to imagine Al Fayed doing a favour for the club and still charging them £1m a year interest, however.

"Looking back, yes I am uncomfortable about the loan we had to take out, but no banks would lend to us," David Davies later admitted. "It was a matter of keeping the club in business." Though the individuals involved with lending money to the club were clearly in charge of a distinctly dodgy past, QPR had to convince the courts that their loan of £10m did not come from any illegal source, and this they managed. The money was considered legitimate and this was when QPR were "allowed" to exit administration. Quite simply, however, if QPR were not to continue to meet their interest payments, their ground would be taken away and a Panama based corporation would have the rights for doing whatever they wished with both the ground and the land. Today Englefield is still the legal advisor whom the club deal with in order to make their regular monthly payment of £83,333.

The connections with football agents becoming investors continued with QPR when Gianni Paladini bought a 14.7 per cent stake in QPR in April 2004. Paladini invested £650,000 in the club and suggested more was to follow. Paladini replaced Bill Power on the QPR board after his significant investment and it was reported that the board were then consulting other groups of investors about buying stakes in the club. Paladini, a Napoli born businessman, had previously been the agent that oversaw high paying deals for Fabrizio Ravanelli, Juninho and Benito Carbone (famously it was the high wages of Carbone, in particular, whilst playing for Bradford City, which brought the club crashing down the divisions when they could not sustain their Premiership aspirations, consequently losing millions and going into administration). Formerly a promising footballer, Paladini was on the books of Napoli where he wore the famous number ten shirt, but had to give up the game due to injury when he was just 18. He then became an interpreter before settling into work as a football agent.

In 2003 he almost took over at Port Vale but the deal fell through and Paladini moved on to QPR. It was claimed by Paladini that he remortgaged one of his homes in order to invest in Queens Park Rangers. After the ABC debacle had been revealed, and the performances of QPR had still not risen above the mediocrity the team had displayed for years, fans were becoming restless and many felt Paladini was a corruptive, draining influence on the club. In short, many were suspicious about his plans for QPR. There followed a series of bizarre incidents, which paint Paladini as eccentric at best and dangerous at worst. Before the beginning of the first game in the 2005/06 season, where QPR were playing Sheffield United (who at the time were managed by current QPR manager Neil Warnock), Paladini was in the chairman's suite. Here he bumped into David Morris, the owner of a 2 per cent stake in the club. Morris asked to have a private word with Paladini, at which point, Paladini later told Blackfriars Crown Court, he was led into the chief executive's office and was surrounded by a group of masked men. Paladini claimed he was "terrified" and had been held at gunpoint by the gang, one of whom – with a gun to his head – insisted, "Sign, sign the paper

- we'll kill you." Paladini claimed he was forced to sign several documents confirming his resignation from his position on the board and handing over his stake in the club. The police and several armed officers arrived at half-time at which point they arrested David Morris and several other men who were still in the offices at Loftus Road. Bizarrely, by the time police questioned Gianni Paladini, the second half had begun, and as Rangers's Marc Bircham scored a goal, Paladini flew away from the interview to run into the directors' box in order to celebrate the goal.

Some questioned the validity of Paladini's statements; several men were charged with conspiracy to commit blackmail, false imprisonment and possession of a firearm. Ultimately, however, all those charged were found not guilty. The documents which Paladini claimed he had signed were never found.

Paladini was no stranger to making threats himself. After several high profile incidents where he fell out with Rangers's manager Ian Holloway, Paladini was, at one point, accused of threatening to kill Holloway. He later admitted this, but claimed it was "in a funny way, and it didn't mean anything at all".

There was also the exceedingly coercive way in which Paladini ousted Bill Power (as well as chief executive Mark Devlin) from the QPR board. It was said that, with two Monaco based companies in tow as well as former World Cup winner Dunga, and football agent Antonio Caliendo (whose clients include David Trezeguet), Paladini "persuaded" Power to resign from his position. Along with his personal team of investors, who bought Power's 19.5 per cent stake, it led to Paladini owning almost 70 per cent of the club which was enough for "total control" of Queens Park Rangers.

The mysterious Monaco based consortiums were Wanlock and Barnaby holdings, suggesting inevitable tax references. It also brought to attention the bizarre truth that Queens Park Rangers, a London based club with bags of tradition, were now owned by an increasingly motley collection of individuals with ties to Italy, Monaco, Switzerland and Panama. Where was the tradition or passion in that? With all of their backers' implausible and indefensible shady dealings, was there even a defence of those individuals passing a Fit And Proper Persons test? The test is supposed to filter anyone with any history of financial irregularity or ambiguity. There is a significant check list which an individual must pass in order to complete the test. Yet many of the factors involved in the test often seem to be overlooked. It not only makes a mockery of the test, but of the state of football in the 21st century.

Paladini defended his actions, saying, "There are people trying to destroy me but they won't win. My head is held high. We did the right thing at the meeting, it was all done properly." Yet, despite Paladini's often admirable defence of his actions, and his cool, Italian charm, there were simple financial facts revealed which defied logic. During Paladini's reign at the club, QPR paid a remarkable £473,000 in agents' fees, many of them friends and former business associates of the Rangers chairman. Some of the transfers were certainly unlikely to have warranted an agent's fee in any normal circumstances. Marc Nygaard signed for QPR from Italian club Brescia on a free transfer, yet agent Brian Hassell received £60,000 from QPR for the business deal.

After his move from Chesterfield, Ian Evatt's transfer to QPR for £150,000 led to agent Melvyn Eves being paid £40,000 by QPR. Eves is a former footballer who has been involved with the game since his retirement as both an agent and an Independent Financial Advisor. His work with Paladini dates back to Paladini's time as an agent himself, when Eves was "advisor" to his represented players – Ravanelli and Carbone.

"These allegations are stupid," Paladini said of his supposed favours to friends. "They are made by people with no understanding of how football works. If they want to paint a picture of me as a crook, they should find something I have done wrong. In fact, I have done nothing wrong, and they have no idea what they're talking about."

Perhaps Paladini was being candid. It doesn't take much reading between the lines to see that football "works" by deals being made between close contacts or even friends, for which those doing the favour are pleasantly rewarded. The payments are written "officially" as part of the deal in paperwork under club headed note paper. Therefore this declaration can be seen to be all above board and legitimate.

But financial accounts make no detail of the ins and outs behind those payments. The £40,000 can be necessary or it may not be. Either way it can still be listed and listed legitimately. Only those with knowledge of what that £40,000 is for will know if it was truly warranted as a club expense. Those viewing the accounts can only speculate. After several occasions where they were said to have disagreed or argued, Paladini and Holloway parted ways, with Ian Holloway leaving to join Plymouth Argyle. The more official reason behind Holloway's departure after years at Loftus Road was his disapproval of having to sign players he had no interest in, among them Marc Nygaard as well as the Italian defender Mauro Milanese.

In 2007 it was announced that QPR were being sold to Formula One magnates Bernie Ecclestone and Flavio Briatore. Investors Antonio Caliendo and Franco Zanotti were said to have received somewhere in the region of £4m in order to resign from the board – Caliendo having been one of the major investors who prevented QPR from going into administration a second time. Paladini remained as QPR chairman, though essentially withdrew any of his own personal investment, saying he and his investors had gone as far as they could with the club. Briatore's investment company Sarita Capital reportedly paid £1m for QPR shares and also resolved to take on £13m of the club's current debt. Ecclestone was previously linked with a buyout of Arsenal, but decided on QPR and personally acquired 15 per cent of the club. The two Italians also agreed to invest £5m in new players for the team.

The money almost seemed to be a letdown given the financial clout of the men behind the takeover. The question was not so much whether they had the money to invest in the club, but why were they bothering with QPR? Certainly there are the Italian connections, but the backing of the club did not just end with Briatore or Ecclestone. A month after their bid for the club had been accepted, Lakshmi Mittal – a steel maker who is the fifth richest person in the world – purchased a 20 per cent share in Queens Park Rangers. New appointments on the Rangers board included Flavio Briatore, Bruno Michel and Alejandro Agag.

The details behind the latter indicate just how powerful the current structure behind QPR is in terms of wealth and prestige. Agag was named as one of the top ten most influential figures in the Spanish economy by the *Financial Times* in 2007. Agag's wedding to Ana Aznar Botella was attended by Tony Blair, as well as the King and Queen of Spain and numerous big name celebrities. At just 28 years of age, Agag was elected as an MEP and moved to Brussels where he was later nominated as Secretary General of the European People's Party. Agag was linked to Formula One, given he has played a key role in expanding the sport throughout Spain, where TV audiences have tripled over the last decade. In 2001, however, Agag announced he was leaving politics in order to focus on his business interests, one of which became QPR.

QPR's finances made perilous reading at the time of the F1 takeover. Their overall loss for the year before was £3,34m (the previous year it had been £2.5m). The club's total debts had increased from £17.2m to £20.7m. This was despite an improved turnover close to £10m. Nevertheless, the club took out further loans from Rangers's directors which amounted to £2.7m and they also ran up a tax bill of £2.6m. Their administration expenses were extensive, running close to £3.5m. This profligacy unsurprisingly had a negative impact on the support of the club. Fans were unconvinced that the club was being run correctly and they showed this by boycotting Loftus Road; the club's average attendance was down by almost 3,000 spectators and the club sold 8,056 season tickets compared to 10,669 from the year before.

Given QPR's ridiculous debts, was it justifiable for Laksmhi Mittal – who is worth close to £20bn – to invest just £200,000 in the club to secure a 20 per cent stake?

Mittal set a new world record for a private home when he paid £70m to Bernie Ecclestone for a house in Kensington Palace Gardens (the former Filipino embassy), which was purchased for his daughter Vanisha. Mittal also sought to purchase the house next door for his son Aditya, for a reputed £117m, though the deal fell through. One of Mittal's own residences, also in Kensington, is decorated with marble taken from the same quarry as that which supplied the Taj Mahal.

Between them, Bernie Ecclestone and Flavio Briatore are worth several billion pounds, yet QPR are seemingly being run with the same abandon as they were before the takeover. What is the benefit to running Queens Park Rangers, a team that has, since the buyout in 2007, finished 14th, 11th and 13th in consecutive seasons in the Championship? Such baffling mediocrity, with little financial profit from footballing activities, seems like a sure fire failure for such world renowned business men. What do they want with QPR? There of course may be an argument for intending to buy a club at a low ebb, build it up and then make a fortune if the club should reach the Premier League, or even a Cup Final. Not only would this appear to be unlikely, even with a seasoned manager such as Warnock in charge, but even if this were the intention, would there not be a great amount of investment? Furthermore, would the ownership of the club really be split so perilously between fellow wealthy men? Any of the owners could buy the club outright and have any future profits to themselves, as well as any potential glory. Equally, whether the ownership is split or not, each and every investor can afford to put in a staggering amount of money, money that would be welcomed by Neil Warnock, who could then increase the club's potential with better quality players. The QPR squad, as has long been the case, is an assortment of young players who did not take off with their first club and journeymen pros who are unlikely to ever hit the league's top scorer or most assists charts.

It seems likely, as has been rumoured, that Lakshmi Mittal is intending to ultimately buy out the other part owners of the club and currently is merely testing the waters as to how to invest and run a football club. To this end, Mittal placed son-in-law Amit Bhatia on the board as the family's representative. Bhatia was named vice-chairman of QPR Holdings Ltd.

Mittal, like so many before him who have become involved with Queens Park Rangers, is no stranger to controversy or questionable business practices. He has been accused of slave labour by some of his employees. His company ArcelorMittal has bases in over 60 countries where it employs some 280,000 people. Mittal was also involved in a scandal alongside Tony Blair, known as "Cash for influence" or "Garbagegate", where Blair aided Mittal in acquiring the Romanian state steel industry. In a letter to the Romanian government Blair hinted that Romania would have a "smooth" entry into the European Union if they allowed Mittal to create a steel monopoly in the country. In the letter to Romanian Prime Minister Adrian Nastase, Blair described Mittal as a "friend". Mittal was revealed to have donated £125,000 to the Labour Party after this favour.

On 19 Friday February 2010, it was announced that Flavio Briatore had stepped down as chairman of QPR Holdings Ltd, and had been replaced by Ishan Saksena. The 31-year-old investment banker had met Amit Bhatia (who married Vanisha Mittal) at Cornell University in New York. After graduation, Saksena worked for ten years in the finance sector, principally in private equity, mergers and acquisitions. Saksena and Bhatia remained in contact throughout that time and, after moving to England in 2007, Saksena was invited to join the board as an adviser, before quickly ascended to chief executive. Once Briatore left the QPR board, Mittal sought to keep it in the family and promoted his son-in-law to chairman. It has to be said that Saksena has talked a good game, recognising prudence and cautious planning should be at the base of any plans to move QPR forward to their former heights. He has also endeared himself to the team itself, appearing in the dressing room and apparently inspiring the Rangers to beat Doncaster Rovers. Perhaps, eventually, the reserve of an investment banker may benefit QPR. It could certainly not come any lower than their plight under Ecclestone and Briatore.

Saksena's appointment followed Briatore's Formula One scandal where he was involved in allegations of race fixing. He was forced to resign as team principal of Renault. His ban was later overturned but Briatore insisted he would not return to F1. It seemed also that he would not return to Queens Park Rangers as an investor with any sway, though he remained a shareholder.

Bernie Ecclestone, however, remains involved in both Formula 1 and affairs at QPR. In another unsurprising connection, Ecclestone has also been linked with Tony Blair and the Labour Party, as well as the European Union. In 1997 Ecclestone was involved in a political controversy over tobacco sponsorship. It was the Labour party's new policy to forbid the advertising of tobacco products though it later recanted in order to allow Formula One cars and drivers to continue their advertising of tobacco products. Bernie Ecclestone then personally donated a million pounds to the Labour party.

In an interview with *The Times*, Ecclestone dropped a clanger of Prince Phillip proportions when he entered into an unsavoury dialogue. "Terrible to say this I suppose, but apart from the fact that Hitler got taken away and persuaded to do things that I have no idea whether he wanted to do or not, he could command a lot of people able to get things done," Ecclestone said. "If you have a look at a democracy it hasn't done a lot of good for many countries – including this one." Ecclestone has been friends with Max Mosley for 40 years.

Mosley is the son of Oswald, a renowned fascist who served as an MP for virtually every political party of any note. Mosley had been leader of the BUP (British Union For Fascists) and his son at first followed in his footsteps, working for the Union Movement as well as the Conservative Party though found it difficult to "get on" with the fascist stigma attached to the Mosley name, a stigma incidentally which did not prevent the naming of particular streets after Oswald Mosley – one of which serves as a main throughway in Manchester city centre. Bernie Ecclestone claimed his friend Max would do a "super job" as Prime Minister, adding worryingly that he didn't "think his background would be a problem". Incidentally, the Union Movement advocated a central Europe many decades ago, a theme of course prevalent to the European Union of today.

Slave labour, fascism approval, can this really be termed fit and proper? Whatever happened to the running of a football club out of love and passion for the game? Whatever happened to local business links and striving to give the fans entertainment and value for money? The dichotomy could not be greater between the management of certain football teams and the ownership behind the scenes. QPR are no exception. You have the gritty, Yorkshire-hewn working-class passion for football that epitomises Neil Warnock, a lifelong Sheffield United fan and football purist.

Inheriting a team of also-rans would not be what Warnock expected when he almost won an FA Cup with Sheffield United, and nearly managed consecutive seasons in the Premier League. Perhaps he was enticed with pots of gold by the current owners of QPR, but the paradox between the candid, authentic persona of Warnock and the money drooling robots who run the club extremely poorly but somehow seem to retain their financial clout, cannot be underestimated. There is business and then there is football. There is certainly room for the two to mix but under the guise of the present owners of QPR, it seems they are concerned with either running QPR into the ground or expecting to invest heavily enough that they become a world respected footballing franchise, capable of earning a fortune. After all we have seen it would be wise not to bet on the latter.

Sources: *Boardroom Blues, Financial Times, The Independent, BBC, Forbes, Herald Sun, www.qpr.co.uk, This Is London, Evening Standard*

WASTE OF MONEY!

8: TV MONEY GONE MAD AND BAD

"Televised games drive me round the bend. The game as I and the ordinary working men knew it has changed almost beyond recognition. I used to regard it as the rape of football, but after more thought I prefer to call it the prostitution of football, the game 'on the game' since the television people set it awash with money. The fans are deserving of sympathy. They still love it but it's costing them a fortune – not only to watch matches live but often when they watch it from the comfort of their own home." – Brian Clough

Without television, football would be vastly different, of that there is no doubt. In fact, the game would be returned to its original state whereby the only way of watching a match was to be aware of your local team and check local listings, be that posters up around town or newspapers. Players would play for the love of the game and the local adulation – and possibly a write up in the paper. Feedback would be instantaneous and somewhat ambiguous. Did the ball cross the line? Was that really a sending off offence? "Cor, did you see that streaker?" "No I was eating my pie."

This somewhat primitive version of football still exists of course; it is just so undeveloped and unsupported that it is a wonder the teams ever survive. You have to go down and down the non league circuit to find football which is no longer televised. Because, in general, a kick of a ball promotes like nothing else and is a massive feature of television viewing as we know it in 2010. It will most likely only increase. It is not simply the deluge of live football and highlights programmes, even adverts now usurp the circular piece of leather at every available opportunity.

Anything from opticians to car insurers might use a football or players during a match to promote their product, reasoning that the majority of men are so perfunctory that one look at a ball causes them to want to play or watch and, therefore, buy. Somewhere along the line it must work, because these adverts are on the rise.

The television coverage of professional football is vast and overwhelming unless you are a football addict to the point of needing professional help. Premier League, Championship, League One, League Two, non-league, Scottish Premier League, FA Cup, League Cup, Scottish Cup, Community Shield, Women's football, Youth internationals, play-offs – and that's just the domestic game. Most fans would agree that, at least to an extent, it is a positive addition to the game. Whereas the likes of Notts County or Carlisle United were rarely seen on a television screen before the 1990s, today we can be assured that whatever our team, we might see them once a season on TV. Yet, realistically, is this much use to a dedicated fan of a side below the environs of the Premier League? Most teams below the top sides in the country have a fan base who visit the ground on a regular basis, a televised match is not going to dissuade the majority of fans from going to a match for real.

It would appear that the idea of TV coverage to this extent is only about two things – overkill and having the monopoly. If Sky have it, then no one else can. Since 1990 Sky has overtaken the entire television structure in the United Kingdom and a huge part of their campaign has centred around sports, of which football has been the dominant leader. Control the football and Sky knew they would control the people. Well, the men at least. To this end, Sky went on a revitalisation spree, repackaging the way the game was televised and coercing the Premier League revolution.

In 1992 Greg Dyke – who was later director general of the BBC – was in negotiations for the football rights for ITV, but he was to be outmanoeuvred by Rupert Murdoch and his Sky company who were to improve on the ITV offer and begin the Premier League, an initiative which we have been led to believe "revitalised" football. The bid at the time was £302m offered for a five year period, a fee which the BBC and ITV combined could not possibly have matched.

Murdoch realised that it was not just about the money, however. He did not court the big teams alone, he focused on the Premier League chief executive Rick Parry as well as many of the lower clubs, promising that with Sky, their club would be featured in the TV package. Sky would not simply show the big teams. To Murdoch's credit, he certainly was not joking and he has kept to his word in making sure the likes of Fulham and Middlesbrough have received decent television coverage.

In his autobiography, *Inside Story*, Greg Dyke explained that, "Parry had been heavily courted by both [BSkyB chief executive Sam] Chisholm and Murdoch. They'd even flown him to Scotland in their private jet to show him the BSkyB call centre." According to Dyke, Rick Parry later told him that, "'Mr Murdoch was the most impressive man I ever met'."

The revivification of football on television has been well documented and does not require full exposure here. Many of us are old enough to remember football on television before the Sky and Premier League revolution. It is the outrageous sums of money and the reasons why which we are most concerned with, along with the impact of the deluge of coverage and impossibility of discerning crap from diamonds.

It hasn't all been plain sailing for the television networks. Whereas Sky has flourished and extended its coverage and therefore its revenue, some networks are only just still afloat thanks to public funding (like the BBC) and some are no longer in action because of their flagrant spending (look no further than ITV Digital and Setanta).

The cost of TV rights to football matches is well known to be astronomical and by and large TV companies do not bid what they do not expect to recoup or cannot afford. That was until Setanta came along. The Irish company's profligacy affected several companies and most importantly several football clubs. Setanta agreed to pay £392m for two of the six packages of Premiership football rights in a three-year period. But less than a year after the agreement they entered administration.

The ridiculous spending was even further compounded by the fact that Setanta were only showing pay-per-view matches. Sky still had the monopoly on the majority of league and cup matches. Sky's own PremPlus channel had previously shown additional Premier League pay-per-view matches but had folded after six years as few fans were willing to consistently pay for additional matches on top of their regular Sky fees. Despite this revealing move, Setanta decided they could match the funding required to buy individual matches from the Premier League as well as the SPL and other European leagues. The network banked on receiving two million subscribers which they would need in order to break even, but they were soon losing £100m a year with just 1.2 million customers paying for their service. Ultimately the company lost £150m on their football initiative and ceased broadcasting in the UK, entering administration. Their company, which banks in Luxembourg, is still trading in Europe but are unable to televise in Britain.

Setanta's creditors included private equity company Doughty Hanson who were owed a total of £85m, which they had believed was a wise investment. Their total investment had been £213m. Television companies had made and lost large investments before, and it is very surprising those behind Setanta did not take heed from the ludicrous collapse of ITV Digital. The company launched as a pay-TV service in 1998 when they were first known as ONdigital. Three years later they were rebranded as ITV Digital but just ten months after this the service ceases and ITV Digital went into administration. The principal backers of the service were Carlton and Granada television, and all banked on customers switching to digital and paying for the privilege.

The main thrust of ITV Digital's campaign was to enlist Football League clubs (all outside the Premiership) in a three-year deal which promised most clubs an average of £3m in TV revenue. Yet the TV audiences and advertising revenues which the company banked upon failed to materialise and consequently, with the company having lost most of its investment, football clubs were owed £178m in total. ITV Digital had promised a total of £315m in investment, a figure they were powerless to reach without the required viewing figures and advertising income.

After their collapse Greg Dyke said, "there is hardly anyone running a television company today who doesn't think they paid too much". Dyke was incorrect when he predicted that, "no one will pay that much again," however. Altogether ITV Digital received £800 million in investment, with many quite rightly wondering exactly where this money went. According to the company, they needed a further £300m just to break even, though they were losing subscribers almost as quickly as they gained them.

The collapse affected every club within the Football League as all had budgeted to include the ITV investment. Many clubs to whom a few million pounds was vital went into administration – Swindon Town, Bury and Barnsley amongst them. It was the south Yorkshire team who felt the greatest irony. Former Tykes chairman John Dennis was once thought to be so impressive at running a football club, that he was invited by Football League colleagues to give a speech on how best to keep a club solvent. Dennis says:

> "Barnsley were regarded by most of our peers as a prudently run, sensible football club. In my time as chairman we made a profit in 12 out of 13 years and the exception was the year we went into administration. We were accused of being profligate for committing money we hadn't yet received but I have no sympathy for that point of view. It was perfectly reasonable to assume the terms of a properly negotiated contract with a properly constituted company would be honoured."

Barnsley were fortunate in that performances on the pitch meant they regained a lot of income but they were certainly in the minority. The transfer market had essentially collapsed for clubs outside of the wealthiest in Britain and as Dennis said at the time, "Unless they have independently wealthy benefactors, clubs outside the Premiership will still face a battle to balance the books for many years to come."

There are only two establishments which will be able to absorb the losses felt by the likes of ITV Digital and Setanta. One is the BBC, who are fortunate enough to be kept alive by public funding, and the second is the perennial money maker, Sky. Rupert Murdoch has a personal wealth of around £4bn and is the 117th richest person in the world, yet it is his company which he is most famous for and which, thanks to far reaching subscription fees charged to the British public, he can count on to afford continuingly excessive TV rights to football matches. Crucially, Sky retain control of the majority of Premier League live matches as well as the unprecedented introduction of full game reruns from the Premier League in their Football First programme which airs every Saturday evening, where viewers have a choice of watching any of the day's Premier League matches. Yet Sky is a one-off, partly because of their immense backing and partly because they took a risk that actually paid off. The only difference is they were able to absorb those early losses thanks to Murdoch.

In the documentary *How TV Changed Football Forever*, Murdoch talks of the gamble he took when he bought the first set of rights for £304m, snatching them away from ITV. "In life, if you're building a company, you've got to take risks. And this was certainly, on the face of it, very risky," he explained. "But I knew from selling newspapers or from television elsewhere that sport is the great, number one common denominator. And, of that, football is number one." At the beginning of Sky's reign over football coverage, the broadcaster was losing £3m a week and all of this was done whilst the establishment was looking down upon Murdoch and his empire. Yet the Australian felt the need to challenge the status quo of televised football.

"I just felt that to be able to give people choice was a wonderful opportunity; to come in and do that, and challenge the sort of BBC establishment," Murdoch explains in the documentary. He adds, "When you're a catalyst for change, you make an enemy of the people that don't want to change. Talk to the BBC, and I'm sort of the devil incarnate, but that's life."

Thanks to the television licence, an unnecessary, superfluous bane on the British public, the BBC has been able to continue broadcasting occasional Championship games as well as the highlights packages and often poorly chosen FA Cup games. Yet this is currently at a cost of £173m to the British public, which is the fee *Match of the Day* has paid for three years of rights, as well as additional internet rights. The BBC also paid an extortionate one million pounds just to broadcast FA Cup matches on its Radio 5Live station. The station's entire budget is a mere £59.1 million and even the BBC trust commented the station had not ensured with "sufficient rigour" that the amount it had bid "represented value for money".

The BBC had paid a similar figure to £173m for their previous five years of football rights but there are few people in the country who do not pay to watch Sky TV and this is reflected in the cost Sky pay the Football League and Association to broadcast an immense amount of live (and highlights of) football.

Overall, out of the six possible football packages available to television broadcasters, Sky won the rights to five and it is surely only a matter of time before they covet all six. Among their haul is an unprecedented right to show

92 live matches. Is it any wonder that we are inundated with advertising for the new season when the last has barely finished? As the last light fades on the previous season we are bogged down by adverts promising live matches from all corners of the globe and the persistent pushing of the Premier League which we are consistently told is bigger and better than ever and the 'best league in the world'. However, the tide is turning, with less top class foreign players deigning to accept the inferior British clubs' wages.

The problem with Sky, as it was with ITV Digital and the Football League, is that the top British clubs are forever indebted to the network's monopoly. They are totally reliant on the money paid to them for their team's matches to be broadcast and without it, most clubs would perish. This is not because they could not make a similar amount of money themselves, but rather that they have become greedy and overspent in so many areas of their business that the TV money is the reliant saving grace which will pay them so many millions for not lifting a finger.

Therein lies the catch-22: Sky needs the major football clubs for its overrated continued coverage and the clubs need Sky's investment, upon which the whole dicey investment behind the current game is precariously balanced. Perhaps, therefore, everyone should be happy. Fans only pay – in money or time – for the games they want to see and the sports package is a choice, not a necessity. Overall, considering the sheer amount of choice and diversity on offer with football coverage, perhaps we should not complain at the service.

Yet the biggest problem caused by the vast sums of money within the game due to television coverage is undoubtedly the fact that the clubs are under more and more pressure to succeed at the highest level in order to sustain the income they so desperately need. The lower down you go, as with the ITV Digital debacle, the harder it is for clubs to adjust to the required levels of spending in order to compete and have any success whatsoever. Most clubs are destined for continued obscurity and an over reliance on television income.

There are mixed messages regarding a small club's rise through the ranks. Take Blackpool for instance, who managed the unthinkable and achieved Premier League status in 2010 after a dream season in the Championship. They reached the play-offs and managed to oust Cardiff City and bag a place in the Premier League. Few people gave them a chance to reach the hallowed ground of the top division in English football (though they were once a staple of the upper echelons). Fewer still would expect Blackpool to finish above 18th in the Premier League by the end of the 2010/11 season. The club has been solvent for many years and the unexpected windfall of Premier League money will only benefit the relatively small, local team. Estimated revenue for reaching the top of the football tree in England is predicted to be some £50n, most of which comes from TV appearances as well as advertising and sponsorship. However, all of this of course, is "predicted" and "expected", it is not guaranteed. It is as abject as predicting that Blackpool will invest heavily in new players and their wage bill will rise exponentially. We could also predict they could over pay and risk remaining in the top league, ultimately heading for administration, like many teams before them.

Blackpool's entire wage bill per year for their relatively humble squad equates to less than £5m, less than most top players' personal salaries in the Premier League.

Can clubs such as Blackpool realistically play with the big boys for anything longer than a season? Are they capable of budgeting in accordance with the money promised to them by the head honchos at Sky? The future of many clubs (any who do not sit comfortably in the top half of the Premier League in fact) is one of dependence and reliance upon Sky television and to some extent, the BBC. As Brian Clough said, it is ultimately the fans who will suffer from the television dominance within modern football. We are now expected to fork out for HD games and 3D coverage, as well as continuing fees for monthly coverage which, during the peak of the season, often equate to at least one live game per night.

We are constantly being told, by Sky of course, just how good their coverage is. Often it is a case of more being better, that because they televise every league under the sun their coverage must somehow be the best. We are often convinced by the tone of a commentator's excited, maniacal voice that we must be equally enthused, that what we are watching is a revelation we must celebrate. The truth is, little happens in most games which last 90 minutes, that's why we all go mad when a goal is scored, because on average there are only two or three goals a game. The incessant need to show replays of every minor incident from every possible angle with the loud, hysterical soundtrack courtesy of commentators who make Children's presenters look like David Frost, is just one aspect of television coverage which is spoiling the game.

Yet we are paying for the privilege of this painful soundtrack and the often pointless, useless "analysis", which now permeates even the most basic television coverage. Watch the previously obligatory *Match of the Day* these days and you will see a scant pick of the "action" from a full 90 minutes. Even the games covered "in depth" will receive five minutes of action and five minutes, or more, of unnecessary "analysis".

How have we allowed this to happen? What has happened to our game that we cannot take back from the money makers? In short we have become unsure of exactly how good the game is, where to go to watch a decent match, who is worthy of our money and who is not. It's easier just to pay our TV licence and Sky subscription and let them dictate what is worth watching.

The future of television broadcasting football matches is most likely set to see an increase of the costs involved; Sky will bid more than anyone else and rates will become even more astronomical than they already are. Perhaps within a year or more, a new bidder will come along in the vein of Setanta and attempt to pry away from Sky their obscene dominance of televised football, but it will be nigh on impossible.

Many will say that Sky has removed the soul from football. In truth the businessmen who were running the game at the time had little soul to steal. It is their greed which led to the domestic channels being pushed out of the arena and gave Sky free reign to take us down the perilous route to which we have since succumbed. The essence of the game is rotten to the core and it is this disregard for tradition or fairness which will see football's eventual collapse. Nowhere is this more prophetic than in the farce which has accompanied television bidding for football games over the last decade.

Sources: *BBC, ITV, Guardian, Daily Mail, Daily Telegraph, Financial Times, Sky Sports, Wikipedia, Football Economy, Four Four Two, Paul Stenning interviews, How TV Changed Football Forever Documentary, Inside Story, Greg Dyke,*

WASTE OF MONEY!

9: THE COST OF SCOTTISH FOOTBALL

"Ludere Causa Ludendi (To Play for the Sake of Playing)" — *Queen's Park FC motto*

Whatever your opinion on Scottish football, whether you are interested in it or not, it is unarguable that the country has a ludicrously one-sided competition. With four main divisions and a total of 42 teams it is laughable to think that just two clubs have dominated the Scottish landscape so stubbornly for the last 25 years. In truth, despite the glory days of Aberdeen and Dundee United in the 1980s and the odd flourish from Hearts, the Old Firm have *always* dominated Scottish football. Between them they have won 94 Scottish League Championships. The irony of this dominance appears in the unfortunate demise of Queen's Park FC, who were the first proper Scottish club.

The team still plays its matches at Hampden Park, an arena which can hold 52,063 spectators, yet often the players run out to echoing voices that total somewhere between two and eight hundred people every week. As if to underline this dichotomy, the club remains amateur in stature, just as they were when they formed in 1867.

A look at the current Queen's Park squad reveals that every single player for the Spiders (so called due to their black and white hooped shirts) is a Scottish native, something a local club can be proud of. However, Queen's Park were something of a market leader as they featured Britain's first Egyptian player, goalkeeper Mustafa Mansour, who played for the club in the early 1930s. They also provided Celtic with Aiden McGeady, the Irishman who played in the youth system for the southeast Glasgow side. McGeady cost the club nothing and they received nothing for his services as he moved into Celtic's youth system before playing for the first-team. Today McGeady would likely command a transfer fee in the region of £5m.

A look at the Celtic or Rangers squads reveals a mere scattering of Scotsmen. So is it right that the main representatives of Scottish football feature very few native players? Few would agree that this is in keeping with tradition yet the Old Firm have always commanded a giant fan base in Scotland and without their quality the league may as well be amateur. To this end, much like England's Premier League, the SPL was formed in 1998, the idea being to highlight the quality of the top 12 teams and leave the three divisions which made up the Scottish League below. These teams now fight it out for what amounts to meaningless competition. *Ludere Causa Ludendi.*

Yet it was impossible for the SPL to counter Celtic and Rangers's dominance. Only Hearts have managed to remove either side from the second position in the league and even in that year – 2005-06 – Celtic were crowned champions. When a player does well for one of the lower ranked sides he will inevitably be snagged by one of the Old Firm. In fact it is more about *which* of them will steal the player than *whether* they will. Derek Riordan played so well for Hibernian that Celtic bought him but after he seemed to lose his zest he was sold back to Hibs. Though Riordan was probably worth something in the region of two or three million pounds, Celtic's derisory offer of £170,000 was accepted by the Easter Road outfit. His return to the club was under cloak and dagger of an 'undisclosed fee'. Kris Boyd was playing so well for Kilmarnock in the 2005/06 season (as he had for the preceding few campaigns) that Rangers signed him during the January transfer window. Boyd shrugged off interest from English Championship clubs and donated his £400,000 signing on fee to Kilmarnock so they could reinvest in their youth set-up, of which Boyd had been a product.

While the occasional selling of home grown players doubtless lifts a club's finances, long-term they have little option but to see their potential stars leave their confines whenever a prospective profit is smelled by Celtic or Rangers. It could be argued that in fact the youth systems of various lower ranked Scottish clubs are merely for the Old Firm's benefit.

One may presume that with their dominance and occasional European flourishes, that Celtic and Rangers are more than financially secure. Yet both are in unjustified levels of debt. Though Celtic regularly rake in profits around the £20m mark every six months, they owe a similar figure to various companies. Ultimately, each year they take to the field, both Celtic and

Rangers are banking on winning the SPL and, ultimately gaining entrance into the Champions League. Without this success they simply add to their debt levels. In 2005 when Celtic threw away the title to their old rivals the 'surrender' was said to have cost the club £4m in 'debt'. This is simply because they are always borrowing against predicted success. Yet why should a club who made £62.5m the year before that mistake, and are considered one of the richest clubs in the world, have a debt of £20m? Should it not be as simple as clearing their debts from their profit and starting from scratch? While they are at it, perhaps they could throw a few million to the third Glasgow side and give Queen's Park a much needed boost.

Martin O'Neill, certainly one of Celtic's most revered managers, was credited with establishing the club on a European scale after their impressive performances in European competition during his tenure. Yet, for all their worldwide support, Celtic are undoubtedly a Glasgow team. Still, the club blame any drop in their profits and increase in their debt on merchandise sales, which tend to falter if the club is not a presence in Europe.

Despite their allure Celtic and Rangers, like their English counterparts, are spending outrageous amounts on transfer fees and wages in order to keep players at the club which will not only win them the SPL but qualify for Europe and maintain their profits. Given the lack of finances for the remaining Scottish clubs and the quite insipid state of the game because of it, it is difficult to feel sympathy for the Old Firm. The big fish in Scotland are small fry outside of its perimeters and can realistically have little hope to ever win a major European competition again. Rangers looked set to remedy a 36-year dearth in Europe when they contested the 2008 Uefa Cup Final but they succumbed to Zenit St Petersburg.

Despite this success, and a recent control over Celtic in the league, the club are in debt to the tune of £31m, a serious amount for a Scottish club. Rangers's finances were so bad in fact that Lloyds Banking Group took control of the club's accounts after it was deemed their spending was out of control. This mini-takeover barred Rangers manager Walter Smith from buying any new players while the finances were assessed and managed.

Jim Murphy, the Secretary of State for Scotland, even demanded assurances from Lloyds that it had not threatened to put Rangers into administration. The club made an outrageous mistake in selling the rights to its shirts and other merchandise to JJB Sports for a one-off payment and has also been hit hard by the collapse of Setanta.

The future seems to consist of a huge restructuring that would enable Rangers (and Celtic) to join a European Super League. So far they have been scuppered in their bid to become part of the English Premier League, with the majority of the English chairmen vetoing the proposed move.

Without this extra income it's difficult to see the situation at either Rangers or Celtic changing. Ultimately it is good for neither the big or small clubs. The Old Firm are forever destined to remain the dominant force in Scotland but mere sprats further afield, with a financial situation that reflects this, while the smaller Scottish clubs flounder under the weight of their own status. It was understandable when former Scotland defender and now manager of Falkirk, Stephen Pressley, commented that those clubs who ran a tight financial ship were being unfairly pushed out by Celtic and Rangers.

Pressley suggested Falkirk have been punished for refusing to live beyond their means. The club's board warned Pressley of financial "Armageddon" if they were relegated. The manager reacted defiantly, saying:

> "Clubs which are operating properly are being punished in the game everywhere. I look at our own club and we are an example in many aspects of how a team's infrastructure is developing young players in the game. We put money into that side of the football club and try to operate with a footballing budget which is correct in how a business should be run."

Comparing Falkirk with the likes of Celtic and Rangers, Pressley commented:

> "You can sometimes suffer from it because of others who spend outwith their means by signing players they really cannot afford. They then rack up unsustainable deficits. That is a form of cheating. We are a good example of a club which is working within its means. Hibernian are also a good example. But yet we both suffer not signing certain players because they are operating in the correct manner."

Rangers manager Walter Smith would not be persuaded into reacting to such comments and was at first adamant that Rangers's debt situation was not a problem. "It is a bit exaggerated," said Smith. "Rangers's debt can be handled by the club. It is a normal business protocol to have a certain level of debt." Referring to the embargo on buying players, Smith tried to smooth the waters, insisting, "I don't think the restrictions are something that, as a manager, you are that conscious of." Perhaps Smith had been convinced, or warned not to talk too openly by the Gers board as just a few months before he had predicted that things were "only going to get worse" for Rangers.

The cost of attempting to live with the big boys was nowhere more evident than in the case of Gretna FC. Gretna is a town so close to England that they would almost have been eligible for the English league. Considering Welsh teams play in the English league there should be no reason why not. Had Gretna been part of the English set-up perhaps they would not now be a defunct club.

Their tale is a lesson in what can happen to a very small club with a lavish owner with pots of cash. Though Brooks Mileson was worth close to a billion pounds when he first purchased Gretna, by the time he withdrew his backing due to illness, Mileson was reportedly hundreds of millions of pounds in debt.

Though Gretna once had a team in the early 1920s, it took until after the Second World War for the club to be properly established when a group of servicemen from world war two formed Gretna Football Club. Ironically, Gretna were indeed counted as an English club for most of their history, playing in the FA Cup and the Northern Premier League. However, they saw their future as a Scottish side, perhaps because this way they would gain greater scope for development and a more specific fan base. After several failed applications, Gretna were finally accepted as a Scottish club in 2002, when, due to their overwhelming debts, Airdrie were unable to continue, which left a space for Gretna.

It was soon after this that Gretna received significant investment from English businessman Brooks Mileson, a truly likeable fellow – as passionate as Sir Bobby Robson and a Mother Theresa to many northern clubs, such as Carlisle United (whom he supported) and Ayr United, whom he had donated countless thousands of pounds to.

Mileson made his money in construction and insurance but longed to be part of a football club. The Sunderland native was adamant it was going to be a northern club, yet felt that just across the border he could help a fledgling club become something great. Gretna seemed perfect. As far as Scottish football was concerned they were something of a novelty and their dilapidated home ground, Raydale Park, reflected that if investment was not forthcoming they would soon be joining other smaller Scottish clubs who barely kept themselves afloat, with low attendances and squads of only home grown players from the local area.

So one day during training, then Gretna manager Rowan Alexander must have thought he was the victim of a prank when a charismatic, eccentric chap offered him £20,000 towards youth development at Gretna. Mileson became owner soon after this with the promise of significant investment into the club, and he developed a key strategy towards rescuing the club from obscurity. For example, he purchased players who were close to retirement and were rotting at big clubs in higher divisions; Mileson believed they could still be useful.

These players were clearly not about to be overawed by their lower division status and when Gretna improved their position and rose up the leagues, those same players were capable of producing on the pitch against the better Scottish league sides. Gretna rose one division, then another and then another. Promotion after promotion and scintillating football was their calling card, not to mention the goals of one Kenny Deuchar. He had previously played for Falkirk but after breaking his leg twice he joined second division side East Fife, whom he played for in his spare time(his full-time job was as a doctor). After a very respectable record for East Fife where he scored almost a goal every two games, Brooks Mileson saw him as exactly the kind of player to steer Gretna to greater heights. He was certainly proved right as Deuchar scored 63 goals in 93 appearances for the club.

As Gretna's profile increased with their fantasy rise through the divisions, Brooks Mileson was often seen helping out in the ticket office, making himself available to staff and fans alike. And when it was time to watch the game, Mileson joined the fans in the terraces. Players were heard to comment that the eccentric owner would often vacuum under their feet during team talks.

Gretna always straddled the line between fantasy and farce, however, with some suggesting Mileson's designs were a little too grand and doomed to failure. He paid his players more than any club outside the SPL and though the town boasted a small population of just under 3,000 the owner planned to build a 6,000 seat stadium. There were the real cynics who also questioned Mileson's motives, intimating that as soon as the team hit the inevitable plateau or struggle, that he would lose interest, or that the club merely served as an egotistical jaunt for a wealthy go-getter. Mileson was adamant that his motives were pure resented his integrity being questioned. "When people say, 'Why is he doing it? What's in it for him?' I resent that," he said. "My wealth, to use that awful word, has been created by dealing with the man in the street, and this is my way of putting something back."

When Gretna reached the final of the Scottish Cup in 2006, losing in a closely fought match via a penalty shootout with Hearts, it appeared Mileson had the last laugh. The following season his side gained promotion to the SPL, a dream ticket.

Yet behind the scenes the club was not entirely solvent, having banked too much on reaching the hallowed land of the SPL where they received less reward than expected. In short, for Gretna to begin to make a profit they would have had to win the SPL and play considerably well in Europe the following season, a ludicrous ask even for the "Good Doctor" (a phrase Sky Sports's Jeff Stelling coined for Kenny Deuchar) and company.

The beginning of the demise for Gretna was the loss of Rowan Alexander. The manager served the club for seven years and was at the helm for every step of their meteoric success. Yet in a strange sequence of events Alexander was refused entry into the club when he arrived to take charge of the team for a match against Falkirk. He was then sacked by the club, but the reasons still seem murky today. One of the reasons appeared to be Alexander's "refusal" to use Pro Zone – a computerised match data analysis system – yet there was no evidence he had been required by owner Mileson to do this and the manager revealed the system wasn't even available to him at certain times anyway. The termination of his contract saw Alexander fight back through the legal system, claiming he was owed £800,000 in wages and that the administration from Mileson's end was sorely lacking; in one incident, he claimed, it took two months for Gretna's HR manager to find a copy of the club's disciplinary procedures.

The loss of his job affected Alexander both personally and professionally and he was unable to find a similar job in senior football. As of January 2010 he became assistant manager at Scottish junior side Glenafton Athletic. "He told me face to face that he would honour everything in my contract," Alexander said in reference to Mileson. Along with the quite puzzling and clearly unfair treatment of Rowan Alexander came the inevitable cutbacks in the youth system at Gretna. This is the first port of call for an owner trying to save money: work on the lowest rung of the ladder. As youth development only affects young players, with only a handful of fans aware of the goings on at this level, it's the first area where an owner can take back some control and trim the purse strings.

Though he was a more personable and arguably more likeable character than the likes of Peter Ridsdale, it has to be said Brooks Mileson was dabbling in the same areas of cost cutting. It was revealed in the spring of 2008 that Gretna had assets worth less than £1m but they had creditors of almost £4m. This included the inevitable bill to the taxman – in this case some £600,000. Also predictable was the HM Revenue And Customs threat that should Gretna not pay their tax bill, the club would be forced into administration.

The familiar process began: club struggling, true debts revealed to be much larger than previously believed, staff at the club reveal lack of wages, club threatened with administration, league does little to stave off the inevitable, club deducted points, cannot possibly remain a profitable business, racks up more debts which it cannot pay and finally becomes defunct.

The details behind Gretna's finances made for sad and sometimes mind boggling reading, however. When the eventual administrators came in to "save" the club, they charged Mileson on average £206.93 an hour for their services, and given the amount of time put into making sense of the financial mess this amounted to over a quarter of a million pounds, which simply added to the club's debt. Interestingly, despite being the owner, Mileson was listed as a creditor, which was due to the fact he had withdrawn his funding for the club a few months before. Mileson claimed to be owed £1.87m, given to the club as a loan in conjunction with his company, Heartshape Limited, which he solely owned. Essentially it appeared Mileson had known the state of the club's finances, but had lost control of how to do anything about it. He withdrew his ownership in the hope of perhaps receiving some compensation from his vast investment. Who exactly could have compensated him is another matter, given he was at the helm for all the club's financial dealings for the past few years. The eventual creditor list for Gretna revealed that Mileson invested almost £8m into the club, £6m of which was used to purchase almost all of the club's issued shares through company WB Newco Limited.

All of this financial melee was going on when Gretna were still an SPL club, destined for relegation to Scottish division one. But as their status was with the Scottish Premier League the governing body had to make some sort of effort to help the club and to this end they donated £100,000 to enable the club to keep going. In some reports this figure was thought to be slightly higher, some claim it was even £250,000. Regardless, though it enabled Gretna to play their remaining fixtures, it was little use to the club long-term.

It was mooted that a new buyer could resolve all of these problems, clear the club's significant debts and give them a new lease of life. Yet ultimately who would have been enough of a gambler to cover almost £4m in debts, as well as new investment, for a team destined to play in a division with an average gate of 2,000?

Perhaps only Brooks Mileson himself might have entertained that idea, and he was ill, suffering from a brain infection. This was additional to his other severe ailments which included a chronic bowel condition and ME. Mileson was too ill to attend any of the hearings relating to Gretna FC. A doctor's letter confirmed that he was so ill that he was having difficulty expressing himself and understanding questions.

The published list amounted to 139 known creditors, which included two former players. James Grady was owed £20,000, while Martin Canning was owed £9,000. Several football clubs were also listed as creditors, including Celtic, Birmingham City, Blackburn Rovers, Barnsley, Sheffield United, Everton and St Johnstone. It was Motherwell who were the biggest creditor of the football clubs, being owed £44,000 which was due to a ground share agreement Gretna requested when Raydale Park was not deemed to be up to SPL standard.

There was also a clue as to why the Gretna youth system had been disbanded. It was revealed that the club owed the University of Cumbria £74,000 which came from the unpaid bills relating to the Gretna youth academy who were based at the university's facility in Penrith.

It would be easy to presume Mileson was some kind of Roman

Abramovich to the little club from southwest Scotland, and perhaps he really was a loveable character who ignited a massive period of success that the club would surely never otherwise have seen. He has to be credited with living a dream and allowing many fans and other observers of Scottish football to live a vicarious dream too. To dare to take on the might of Celtic having only been a minnow a few years before; to push Hearts all the way in the Scottish Cup Final.

Hearts were a team who had their own eccentric owner. Vladimir Romanov took over the club in 2005 when they were on the verge of collapse. Since then he has been through 12 managers and once threatened the whole team with transfer to "Kilmarnock, or any other club that will take you".

When Gretna could not even convince the Scottish League that they were capable of surviving in the second division they were demoted to the third, but when a new takeover bid did not materialise Gretna were forced to resign from the football league altogether. The administrators announced they were looking to sell the Raydale Park ground and that it was unlikely it would be used for football. Gretna had no ground, no staff, no players (they had all been absolved of their obligation to the club) and on 8 August 2008 the club were formally dissolved. A group of supporters founded Gretna 2008 in response and Annan Athletic replaced Gretna in the Scottish third division.

On the morning of 3 November 2008, 60-year-old Brooks Mileson was found unconscious, lying in a pond on land at his home in Blackford, Cumbria. He was taken to a local hospital but pronounced dead on arrival. The exact cause of his death is still a mystery.

Mileson had his own creditors, 139 to be precise, and a figure of £8m remained outstanding at the time of his death. It was later reported that just £2m of his estimated £32m fortune could be traced. Mileson's "hidden assets" were reported to include foreign and domestic properties as well as secret trust funds. He did not leave a will and in a cruel twist, Mileson's wife Geraldine and their daughter Helen were made homeless when his Blackford estate was repossessed. The former tycoon, once Britain's 37th richest man, was reported to be so poor in his final days that he could not afford to pay his monthly £47 Sky TV bill or the council tax.

It was a tragic end to the whole sorry saga. Whatever the details behind the financial dealings at Gretna, there can be no question that Brooks Mileson loved football and sought only to create a successful club where there had previously been none, for people in an area which had been seriously neglected as far as football was concerned. He was certainly a philanthropist, and was perhaps only curtailed when it became clear his ambition outweighed his finances and his experience of running a professional football club.

The *Scotsman* summed up the Gretna story succinctly, when it printed this analogy:

> Once upon a time there was talk of a Hollywood movie: an epic tale of the rise of the underdog and of a miracle achieved through faith alone. Think Field Of Dreams meets Seabiscuit, set against a backdrop of wedding rings, anvils and football.

Two years on, the story of the rise and fall of tiny Gretna FC still has enormous cinematic potential – but as a bleak, Ken Loach-style drama about self-delusion and thwarted ambition.

The case of Gretna certainly does not give those who control Scottish football a favourable reputation. Is there an unspecified desire to only let the smaller clubs go so far? Furthermore, is Scottish football doomed to fail? It seems that without a ridiculous investment into another club – billions as opposed to millions – then no one is ever going to challenge the Old Firm. Yet when even those two formidable forces are struggling under debt, doesn't the future look bleak?

In the 2009/10 season, Ross County of the first division, who could only manage mid table in the league, reached the final of the Scottish Cup where they met Dundee United, a team replicating their 1980s thrust, chasing Celtic for second spot in the SPL. Ross County had had the proverbial fairytale run in the cup, beating Hibernian in the quarter-final before disposing of Celtic 2-0 in the semi-final. Such giant killing exploits at such a crucial stage of the competition, not just the third round, certainly bode well for the excitement and opportunity still possible to the lower league sides in Scotland. Ross County unfortunately lost 3-0 in the final.

But one competition is not going to change the firmly established rot at the top of the game. It's something Stephen Pressley has seen first hand as his Falkirk side – who could have played in the Europa League in the 09/10 season but failed to qualify – limped to the end of their season, finishing bottom of the SPL.

Commenting on the domination of the Old Firm on Scottish football's finances, The Bairns's gaffer said, "I don't know how you can sort it out – maybe you could introduce salary caps or have wages in relation to your turnover. Something needs to be done to have it addressed. It is up to the SFA to take action on such a thing."

Sources: *The Scotsman, The Herald, BBC, The Cumberland News, Times Online, News & Star, The Daily Record, Daily Telegraph, Scotland On Sunday, Mail On Sunday*

10: SCANDAL AND DEBACLE
LIFE AT PORTSMOUTH FC

"I've not only got to sell the club, I've got to sell it to the right people." – Andrew Andronikou

Portsmouth has always been a rather unique club; whether it be the bizarre financial structure or the persistent bell ringing which accompanies every match home and away. Throughout their history they have enjoyed periods of unfettered success and numbing mediocrity. Through it all they have always maintained a solid fan base and a likeable style which is often easy on the eye. In short there is nothing to dislike about Portsmouth, they are simply a solid, reliable footballing club. Or at least they were.

The club was formed in 1898 and have always called Fratton Park their home ground. After many years in the old second division the club won promotion to the top division where they initially struggled, but after the break which was installed during the Second World War the club won the English league in 1948/49 and 1949/50. They had also enjoyed a fruitful ten-year period where they were a strong force in the FA Cup. They were runners up to Bolton Wanderers in 1929 and five years later they were back at Wembley, beaten by two late Manchester City goals. In 1939 the club finally won their first FA Cup, beating Wolverhampton Wanderers 4-1.

This was a memorable Portsmouth side that contained the likes of John Anderson and Cliff Parker who both had superb scoring records for the south coast side.

Interestingly, given their current plight, Portsmouth were on the verge of bankruptcy in November 1976. The club were in debt amounting to £25,000 and were saved by supporter contributions, fans who had read of the club's dire finances via *The News*, a local newspaper. The club also had to sell their best players in order to remain solvent. They relied on young, inexperienced players as well as a new manager in the form of former Motherwell player and manager (and future *Saint and Greavsie* presenter) Ian St John. During their struggles Pompey were ultimately relegated to the fourth division just two years after their debt problems were announced.

Though not directly related to future problems, this was really the beginning of Portsmouth's struggle to remain consistent as a club. With a rollercoaster ride during the 1980s and 1990s the club managed to reach an FA Cup semi-final where they only lost in a penalty shootout, and were up and down divisions, unable to stabilise their team or management.

The real turn in the tide began in 1996 when Portsmouth appointed former England manager Terry Venables as director of football, a term which was then relatively unheard of and still remains vapid and inconsequential now. Venables, who has certainly had more than his fair share of questionable appointments and roles in a variety of ultimately negative situations, later became chairman, having purchased a 51 per cent stake of the club for the princely sum of £1. Venables, who was also Australia manager (for which he was paid £200,000 a year) at the same time of his Portsmouth efforts, was his usual cheeky self, flooding the Pompey squad with underachievers from the southern hemisphere. Venables was often in Australia and Portsmouth suffered poor results. Likewise, Australia, who lost to Iran and consequently failed to qualify for the 1998 World Cup. Into just his second season at Fratton Park, Venables was unpopular with supporters, and decided to leave the club along with then manager Terry Fenwick. Venables sold his stake in Portsmouth to Pompey director Martin Gregory, the son of former chairman, Jim. Confusingly, John Gregory (no relation) was also manager of the club in the late 1980s.

At the time Venables sold his stake in the club, Pompey were reported to be losing £150,000 a month. There was difficulty in paying players and staff, with the PFA eventually stepping in to resolve the issue. Despite the problems in the Pompey board room, Venables's company Vencorp were paid £300,000 by the club just three months previously, a payment which was termed a "one-off performance bonus".

Venables made £299,000 on his investment, accepting a gratuitous pay-off from Martin Gregory and walking away free of responsibility, with Portsmouth rumoured to be of interest to an American business consortium. Though it may have seemed on paper that El Tel made a significant and pleasing profit on his time at Pompey, the Guv'nor was most likely disappointed. After his tremendous work with England, where the national team reached the semi-finals of Euro '96, Venables expected that in buying a popular club he would attract significant investment interest which would enable him to make millions from a deal. But during his 11 months at the club no investment was forthcoming and Venables was forced to wait. Shortly before he accepted a £300,000 buyout figure, Venables had been offered £200,000 which he declined. It was reported by the *Independent* that he was banking on a figure closer to half a million.

At the time of his leaving Portsmouth Venables was in and out of court, with the Department of Trade and Industry seeking to have him disqualified as a company director as a result of his involvement in other companies in the past. Whilst at Tottenham Hotspur as chief executive between 1991 and 1993 Venables was ousted by his fellow directors. After a brief reinstatement from a temporary injunction, he was removed by the High Court and ordered to pay costs. This was due to mismanagement of four companies, one of which was Tottenham. Venables was accused of "bribery, lying and deception", three similarly gross descriptions which suggested his "butter wouldn't melt" "image" was exactly that. In September of 1993, BBC's *Panorama* programme alleged various misdealings had occurred which were connected to Venables' businesses. El Tel responded by offering money to charity if the BBC could prove their allegations, also threatening libel action against the programme.

Things now began to cloud over at Portsmouth. In 1998, during Pompey's centenary season, the club announced they were in financial crisis and in December that year the club went into receivership. At the end of the season Portsmouth narrowly escaped relegation, and they were taken over by Milan Mandaric who became new chairman and saved the club from closure.

In 2002 after the club had employed Graham Rix as manager, a spell of poor results lead to the director of football, Harry Redknapp, taking over team affairs, working alongside Peter Storrie, a friend from his days with West Ham. Redknapp is a long time associate of Terry Venables, and Redknapp himself is no stranger to controversy or corruption allegations. The lines at Portsmouth were beginning to join and, in so doing, were mapping their inevitable downfall. Redknapp had two spells in charge of Portsmouth and both were wracked with controversy and intrigue. The details of this could certainly fill a separate book and here it is only pertinent to remember that Redknapp was investigated by, coincidentally, *Panorama*, for "tapping up" Blackburn's Andy Todd, although this was perhaps a case of coercion where Redknapp failed to be enticed. Redknapp was, however, arrested on suspicion of conspiracy to defraud and false accounting, along with Portsmouth's chief executive Peter Storrie and Milan Mandaric.

A spokesman for the club said that:

> "[Storrie and Redknapp had] been asked to help police with their inquiries concerning a matter dating back to 2003. This was prior to the new owner taking control of the club at the beginning of 2006. The club is fully supportive of Peter and Harry who are co-operating fully with City of London Police in this ongoing inquiry. Both are playing major roles in the continued success of Portsmouth Football Club."

Redknapp himself was seemingly unaware of any wrongdoing – the butter certainly not melting anywhere in the vicinity of the Londoner. Redknapp said, rather unconvincingly, that:

> "We all helped the police with their inquiries, but it doesn't directly concern me, it's other people involved. I've been answering questions to help the police. I am not directly concerned with their inquiries. They have to arrest you to talk to you, for you to be in the police station. I think that's the end of it, it didn't directly concern me."

As part of the corruption enquiry, Harry Redknapp and Milan Mandaric are currently both being investigated for allegedly cheating HM Revenue & Customs out of £200,000. This relates to a payment Mandaric had made to Redknapp through a Monaco bank account. It is also interesting to note that Redknapp had previously denied any wrongdoing with regards to tax evasion. A statement from Redknapp's solicitor said before the revelation of his tax avoidance, "Harry Redknapp is extremely surprised and disappointed to have been informed that HMRC intend to institute proceedings against him in the week commencing 11 January 2010. We believe that the decision to commence proceedings will, in due course, be shown to have been totally misconceived." Willie McKay, who worked with Tedknapp as a football agent on many deals, was also charged under the proceedings.

Peter Storrie was also charged under counts of tax evasion, relating to the transfer of Amdy Faye from Auxerre to Portsmouth in 2003 whereupon no tax was paid on the signing-on fee Faye received. Other than this it must be said that despite the investigations and miles of newspaper column inches that accompanied the Redknapp saga, the Pompey manager was ultimately released without charge, threatening to take the police to court over his arrest. It seemed to be, however, that the incidents were not completely fictitious, rather that they couldn't be proved. Or, just as likely, that certain key players in the death of a football club were given free rein to continue as before. If not, then why are these same characters still continuing within the game, as new allegations continue to crop up? Why are the same names involved again and again in football at the deepest, darkest level? Moreover, why are these people allowed to have positions of authority and power at the helm of a football club when they have been even remotely linked to such corruption?

Redknapp and Venables are long-term associates; they even appeared together in an advert for *The Sun* newspaper, backing England's campaign to win the 2010 World Cup. The connections are plain to see between Venables and Redknapp and centre particularly around Tottenham and Portsmouth. Perhaps this may be perceived as a tenuous link yet there are certainly many parallels between the two. In October 2008, Redknapp was granted "Freedom of the City" of Portsmouth, which received an unsurprisingly mixed reception by Pompey fans given Redknapp had, only two days before, left to join Tottenham as manager.

In December 2005 Portsmouth football club was part-purchased by French businessman Alexandre 'Sacha' Gaydamak – in a deal which was "helped along" by Pini Zahavi. Zahavi clearly believed initially that he had made a positive deal for Pompey, saying:

> "Portsmouth were on the way to crash down, not to the first division, but to the second or third. All I did was manage to bring somebody who could put his own money into the club. Show me one club in England run

by totally British people that is not a business. Of course,
a football club is a business that serves the community,
but it is still a business."

The Gaydamak family is very wealthy and influential, with Alexandre's Russian-Israeli father Arcadi the owner of Beitar Jerusalem FC. Initially Gaydamak became co-owner of Portsmouth along with Milan Mandaric, yet this was soon turned over to Gaydamak completely with Mandaric remaining as non-executive chairman for several months. Portsmouth were then owned through Gaydamak's Devondale Investments, a company based in the British Virgin Islands, and Belvia S.a.r.l. one of his businesses based in Luxembourg. Doubtless there were some advantages tax-wise to having companies based in these locations. After several years of fairly mediocre football and little revealed publicly about Pompey's finances, Gaydamak agreed to sell the club to Sulaiman Al Fahim in July 2009. It would later become known that Gaydamak appeared to have sold many of Portsmouth's assets as well as running their mounting debts higher and higher. Despite this, on the surface at least, Portsmouth had no bigger debt than a club the size of, say, Swansea.

The arrival of Gaydamak seemed exciting to begin with, somewhat on a par with the Russian evolution at Chelsea. He promised £15m of initial investment which saw players such as Benjani (who cost a club record £4.1m) and Pedro Mendes arrive at Fratton Park. In the first full year of Gaydamak's ownership, Portsmouth lost £1 million after just staying in the Premiership. Their player wages were a sizeable 68 per cent of their total revenue. A million pounds of debt, however, was controllable. The next season saw an increase in salaries; £36m of their overall £40m revenue was spent on wages and their loss at this stage was £23m.

One would have thought at this point that Gaydamak or any of his advisors – perhaps one who could use a calculator and a spreadsheet – may have realised the spending was out of control in relation to the income. Portsmouth were never going to challenge for the league title and their best hope of success was almost certainly the league or FA Cup. The higher they could finish in the Premiership, the better their income, but overwhelmingly they had to rely on TV and sponsorship money along with club merchandise sales to fund their growing and bizarre set of wage accounts. Throughout this period the rumours were growing that the real source of power at Fratton Park was not Alexandre Gaydamak, but his father. Sacha always denied this of course, claiming it was "his own money" which was being used to finance Portsmouth.

In 2008, Portsmouth's centenary year, they did indeed win a prestigious trophy when they were proud winners of the FA Cup, beating Cardiff City in a turgid affair that finished 1-0. This was the first time they had won the competition for seventy years. Best of all, they qualified for the Uefa cup for the following season. Yet even in the year where the club reached an unprecedented pinnacle they were still running at a heavy loss. Their wage bill was now £54m and their revenue a worryingly close £70m. Altogether, with bonuses also having to be paid, the club lost £17m that year. Yet still the increases did not stop. Inflation would have been one thing but Portsmouth were expanding their wage empire without the necessary cash in place, to a worrying extent. Despite selling some of their best assets in Jermain Defoe, Peter Crouch and Lassana Diarra, the club were still £13m short of breaking even, with their wage bill a ridiculous 108 per cent of their £60m turnover. Ironically, both Crouch and Defoe joined Harry Redknapp's Spurs side. Crouch is one of several players still owed money by Portsmouth.

Even when the club are now deep in investigation and under administration, they have been running a wage bill that is still 98 per cent of their total revenue – and all this with few players of significant value in the squad. They include half decent players such as John Utaka but any ongoing transfer fee would unlikely reach anywhere near his original cost (£7m) to Pompey.

Overall, during Gaydamak's time at the club they earned £246m in revenue yet their outgoings tipped over £300m. Gaydamak proposed a new stadium and made limited improvements to the club's rented training facilities but seemingly little else other than to plunder them further into their inevitable debt. His investment was based on the aspirations of a top ten finish, which dramatically increased the wages and overheads. After Milan Mandaric left the club, Portsmouth became a limited company, and with Gaydamak at the helm they began to invest heavily in non-footballing businesses such as shopping centres and other local business interests.

Given this, between 2007 and 2008 the club employed almost 400 staff.

In September 2008, during the onset of Britain's financial crisis, Portsmouth, who had been relying heavily on money loaned from various factions, were stunned when Standard Bank reduced their level of lending to the club. In Summer 2007 the South African bank had loaned Pompey £25m. The club's own private bankers, sensing a future meltdown of the club, then demanded to be paid the £5.5m that they were owed.

Peter Storrie would later say:

> "Everything got frozen in Israel. Sacha used Standard Bank in the UK and they got collywobbles. They wanted money repaid. Barclays wanted their money. Sacha told me there were no more funds. 'How the hell are we going to survive?' I asked. 'We have this massive wage bill. There are loads of transfer fees to pay.' I had to find £44 million to pay the banks – plus the players' wages, which were running at £4.5 million a month."

The irony stands that the assets were frozen in Israel when Arcadi Gaydamak was sued by Balram Chainrai and Levi Kushnir, who would later own the club, for money owed to them by Gaydamak.

Standard Bank alone were owed in excess of £20m by Pompey, yet this debt was offset to Ocadia Investments Limited, a corporation controlled by the Gaydamak family trust. It was at this point that Gaydamak sought a buyer for the club, all the while intending to write a large IOU for the £31.5m he claimed he was personally owed by Portsmouth. Peter Storrie entered into negotiations on behalf of Gaydamak, to find a prospective new owner and it was during this process that 32-year-old Sulaiman Al-Fahim, a Dubai property mogul, offered to buy the club. Al-Fahim is unable to return to his homeland after he was arrested for an alleged corrupt property deal, clearing out his Dubai assets and vowing not to return until his name had been cleared. Al-Fahim – whose parents and brother were killed in a car accident when he was 21 – has claimed to have a Ph.D in real estate and is often referred to as Dr. Al-Fahim. He had already attempted to take over Manchester City but ultimately was usurped by Mansour bin Zayed Al Nahyan.

In May 2009 Al-Fahim put forth a proposal to buy Portsmouth and even though, as has since been revealed by the club's administrators, "insufficient proof of funding was provided, the transaction proceeded". He promised to put £60m into the club but ultimately would only provide them with £5m. Al-Fahim sought to fund the purchase via costly debt funding and not through his own personal equity. Yet Al-Fahim has been referred to as the Donald Trump of Abu Dhabi and is ranked 16th in a list of the 100 most powerful Arabs in the world. His personal fortune is said to be somewhere in the region of £60bn. Despite this obscene wealth, Portsmouth were in desperate need of capital as they could not fund day to day trading. Why would Al-Fahim buy the club without instantly erasing their debts and aiming to buy the best players in the world? He could have managed both in a matter of months. Among the club's creditors at the time were HMRC who were demanding a payment of £12.4m, with the total owed to them somewhere in the region of £16m.

Peter Storrie later confessed:

> "We went through September, October and half of November 2009 with no money coming in. The accounts department were fighting fires but people, even the Revenue, were understanding, were helping us. The players were outstanding. Michael Brown, Jamo [David James] and Hermann Hreidarsson said to me: 'Look, we want to help.' I said: 'Can you help by just being paid basic and we hold back your appearance money.' It's about £3,000 a win and £1,500 a draw – times 18 in the squad. They all agreed."

Portsmouth were heavily reliant on investment and stabilising from Al-Fahim yet he soon sold 90 per cent of his shares in Portsmouth to Ali al-Faraj in a deal made through al-Faraj's company, Falcondrone Ltd, of whom very little is known. During the short period Al-Fahim was in charge of the club, he had apparent difficulty in making investment or reducing their considerable debts and sought a temporary loan from Portpin Ltd, a company owned by Balram Chainrai (a Hong Kong property developer) and his Israeli business partner Levi Kushnir. Portpin lent Portsmouth £6.5m and this loan was water tight with several assurances.

The money was secured against Portsmouth's stadium, their future television revenue and al-Faraj's 90 per cent share. The debt soon soared to

£18.5 million, with Sulaiman Al-Fahim watching from behind the scenes where he was now the non-executive chairman of the club. The characters behind Portsmouth's remarkable situation were often shaded in mystery, none more so than Daniel Azougy, a former lawyer in Israel who was certainly involved with the club, it's just that nobody knew to what extent. Club sources did confirm at one stage that Azougy personally negotiated the sales of Younes Kaboul to Tottenham for £5m and Asmir Begovic to Stoke for £3.25m.

Mark Jacob, the London solicitor who became executive director at Portsmouth after the takeover by Ali al-Faraj, was later said to have refused to sign off the Begovic deal because he believed the club should have secured more for the promising 22-year-old. In 2001 Daniel Azougy had been convicted of fraud and deception in Tel Aviv. The report of the 2001 case in the Israeli newspaper *Yedioth Ahronoth* quoted the judge, David Rozen, as saying Azougy was: "A sophisticated lawyer willing to do anything to reach his own personal goals. He lied, cheated, used a forged document and stole money from his clients." Azougy served five months in jail and received a further ten-month suspended sentence. Yet just a year later he was disqualified by the Israel Bar Association and forbidden from acting as a lawyer for 14 years, after he was found guilty of presenting false documents before a judge. Azougy was fined and received another suspended sentence and was also ordered to do several hours of community service.

The reasons Azougy was allowed to be let anywhere near Portsmouth FC were certainly sketchy. The "Fit and Proper Person" test which should have been the bare minimum conducted upon Azougy was never enforced because the league did not believe Azougy's position could be classed as senior. "We have asked numerous times for clarification of Mr Azougy's role," a Premier League spokesman said at one stage. "Each time the board has said he is a consultant on a short-term contract."

But in Tony Husband's documentary, screened in mid 2010 on behalf of BBC south, Dan Johnson, Chief Spokesman of the FA Premier League admitted:

> "It concerned us to the point where we refused to deal
> with him. We had several occasions where he turned up
> to meetings at this very building, Gloucester Place, and
> he was shown the door. We said 'we're not dealing with
> you because you haven't subjected yourself to the Fit

and Proper Persons' test and we have deep underlying suspicions that you are behaving as a director or a shadow director', and we quite simply wouldn't deal with him."

Perhaps because of the lack of information available on Azougy, many saw him as the real source of power, along with Arcadi Gaydamak. There are numerous political links which have been levelled at both Gaydamak and Azougy, enough indeed for a book in its own right. It would not be pertinent to enter into their ties or rumours here, however it is interesting to note that two of the most prominent movers at Falcondrone, Yoram Yossifoff and Roni Maneh, have been linked as high as the US President Barack Obama. Interestingly, in an interview with an Israeli newspaper, when it had been suggested his businesses were in trouble, Arcadi Gaydamak did indeed confirm he was Portsmouth's owner.

After just 40 days with Ali al-Faraj in charge Portsmouth FC was again sold on, with Balram Chainrai taking the reins at the behest of stabilising the club. Once again, Chainrai could have paid for the club debts several times over, in fact he could have bought every single Premier league club several times over. Yet still, the club could not sustain trading and needed £35m to become "sustainable". Administration was an "inevitability, to safeguard their position," according to their administrator Andrew Andronikou. Of course men such as Chainrai are usually careful with their investments and don't like to throw good money after bad, but wouldn't it have been a safer investment long-term if Chainrai had brought the club back to solvency? He personally could have bailed the club out of their player debts; yes they would still have been relegated but with a balance of zero they certainly would have been one of the favourites for promotion the following season.

There could only be one reason why a man like Chainrai would buy the club and still allow them to fall into administration: he still owns the club, and can make more personal profit by not clearing their debts. Allowing the debts to dissolve as they were not created with him in charge, and then taking any future profits or benefits because he is now in charge, seems to be the plan. Take a sleeping, potential giant and name yourself as owner with very little capital risk. It is the equivalent of Terry Venables buying the club for £1, but why has it happened with Portsmouth again?

Pompey owe their former owners some £38m in unsecured loans. Since when did an owner charge his previous company for money lent? Isn't the point of owning a club to take sole responsibility for its affairs? If an owner brokered the deals that led the club to debt why should he be allowed to claim the money back? Ownership of any big business is a risk and the risks and benefits should remain with the owner at the time. As we have seen, the majority of the time owners like to pay themselves or their other companies bonuses for the most innocuous reasons so they should also take the responsibility when the business becomes unsustainable. They should either face the music and derive any possible future benefits, or get out and lick their wounds. A club should not be liable overall for any individual's methods of dealing with club business.

The owners are in fact the ones who seem to escape with their money intact and as usual it is only the club staff and the fans who suffer, although it has to be said that for Portsmouth to not even manage to pay its own players is a ridiculous and unfair situation, which has happened twice on their way to administration.

On 10 March 2010, 85 members of staff at Portsmouth FC were made redundant, while the remaining employees only received a percentage of their wages whilst administration was ongoing. Just five days later, unusually the club was advertised for sale in the pages of the *Financial Times*. Chainrai has maintained throughout Portsmouth's battle with administration that he is not actually the full-time owner of the club and will sell them when in receipt of a reasonable offer. For now he says he is merely protecting his own investment. He most certainly is doing this, charging the club to lease their own ground which would produce a yearly return of around a million pounds.

The credit report for Portsmouth reads like a mockery of how to run a football club. It reveals that from 2007 Portsmouth were operating under an average loss of £7.6m per year. Some of their most revealing expenses included £2m in wages per month, £32,306 on away match travel and accommodation, and almost £50,000 on police services for home matches. They were also paying a fee of £2444.46 per month to Sky, and it wasn't for their satellite dishes. Pompey were also paying £1,040 a month just to print their home match tickets.

Though it was not the bulk of their financial mess, the 15 pages of trade creditors Portsmouth were in debt to make for intriguing and sad reading. There were a vast number of individuals who were owed anything from

£200 to £2500 by the club but there were some unique entries among the throng of people and companies. Pompey owed the Ministry Of Defence £626.92, the local Priory Community Sports Centre £11,000, Queens Park Rangers £3,500 and the South Central ambulance service £19,500.

In 2010 the club owed over £15m on transfer fees and follow on payments for players including Kevin-Prince Boateng, Sulley Muntari and John Utaka. There was £3m owed on "image rights" for certain players, Utaka among them, as well as David Nugent and Niko Krancjar. There was also £10m owed for agents' fees.

Andrew Andronikou, the man tasked with overseeing Pompey's administration, said, "Portsmouth is an example of how not to conduct business in the world of football. If you overspend and don't budget accordingly you cannot rely on money from the owner or the proprietor coming in to bridge the gap, and in that it's no difference to any other business."

Yet HMRC challenged the club going into voluntary administration and questioned the validity of Andrew Andronikou's appointment as administrator. It was claimed that Andronikou may have links with owner Balram Chainrai, compromising his independence. If this were true, it would fit in with the perceived plan behind Chainrai's ownership. Going into administration is effectively the same as becoming self-sufficient; the club is given a reprieve albeit with a more sceptical set of future investors. But if Chainrai was to sell the club to a fellow billionaire, would they really be concerned with a few million pounds clear up operation?

Peter Storrie has been the one constant throughout Portsmouth's financial turmoil, despite the changing nature of his title within the club. Storrie has been director, executive chairman and chief executive officer in his eight years at the club. Storrie was previously a colleague of Harry Redknapp during their association at West Ham United. According to official reports at the time, Storrie's move to Portsmouth – after a brief spell at Notts County – was in order for him to help improve the club's "infrastructure" and to "make recommendations as to the future organisation".

These kinds of roles have long been questioned by the football business sceptic, the very term "director of football", for instance, has long been loathed by anyone with an ounce of footballing integrity. This is because anyone in their right mind can see that this position is mere lip service to the individual concerned. It may either be a way to offer respect to that individual for their previous contribution to a club, or it can be a way to siphon funds to a particular individual whilst seeing that the corruption and bad management at a particular club can continue. Wherever you look, the more comings and goings in these positions, the more financial turmoil is usually affecting the club concerned. Andrew Andronikou admitted that Storrie, "was a senior officer of the company and the company has failed so it goes without saying that yes he must bear a large part of the responsibility, absolutely." Yet there was also the assertion that Storrie had, "exercised his judgement to try to save the club at all costs".

"All costs" is certainly a pertinent phrase. It has to be said, with no bias against Storrie, that surely in his role (call it what you want, he was in a very high-profile responsible role at the club), he should have flagged up the problems much sooner and not allowed the club he has often been quoted to say he loves get to such ridiculous financial depths. The Pompey fans have long been suspicious of a director who is paid a basic salary of £600,000, with untold additional extras. After their 2008 cup win, Storrie was paid a bonus of £750,000 by Sacha Gaydamak (his basic at the time was a mere £450,000). Though Storrie would undoubtedly claim he did well in Portsmouth's very respectable 2007/08 season, football purists would ask exactly what position did he play in during Portsmouth's cup winning season. A bonus of three quarters of a million pounds, for a team that essentially had nothing to do with him, winning a competition, has to be seen as ridiculous in any walk of life.

For Storrie to accept this knowing the club was in serious debt has been questioned by the fans from the beginning. Even Storrie admitted that the amounts of bonuses and add-on fees concerning their players was ludicrous and it put the club in a very awkward position. "I never thought it would happen. We had it on John Utaka with Rennes. The FA Cup final cost us £3-4 million. I got calls from clubs saying: 'Congratulations! Pay us the add-ons!'" Despite this, Storrie still accepted his personal bonus.

Worse still, with their problems worsening on the balance sheet, in January 2009 Gaydamak again paid Storrie a bonus, this time of £500,000. Let's not forget, this is almost his entire yearly salary – in one month. According to Storrie he had brought in "an awful lot of money" and this was why he was paid a bonus, but is it logical for a director who loves the club to help reduce its debts and then accept a windfall of half a million pounds? That money could have paid the local ambulance service for life. Storrie claims that due to "cashflow problems" he did not take the money until seven months later ... when Portsmouth were accruing even greater levels of debt. Even worse, despite not pulling on a pair of boots in any of Pompey's matches, Storrie was included in the players' bonuses for a win or a draw. If the team won he received over £3,000 and even if they limped to a tepid 0-0 Storrie still picked up £1,500 – even when Michael Brown and co did not receive theirs. Incidentally the bonuses included not only those promised to players for reaching Europe, but to other clubs if players signed from them won them a trophy or qualified for Europe – clauses which were agreed when either outcome seemed unlikely. The other clubs were in contact very quickly after the win over Cardiff. David James remembers being told, "This will ruin us", by someone at the club when Pompey won the FA Cup.

Storrie has admitted that he should have been "stronger" in persuading Gaydamak that he wasn't Roman Abramovich and that he certainly couldn't run a club like him. Despite Gaydamak's heavy personal fortune, Pompey were in the mire and Storrie was very aware of it. Storrie told the *Daily Telegraph*:

> "The mistake I made was I should have been even stronger with Sacha and said: 'If you're going to carry on doing this I'm off.' Harry wanted to build a big, great side and you don't have the likes of Sol Campbell, Lassana Diarra and Sulley Muntari playing down at Fratton Park unless there's big money. Clearly the income from the club couldn't get anywhere near that. Several times the board and I pointed out that 'we are way, way overspending here'."

Storrie has an unfortunate knack of painting himself as a naive accomplice in a situation he had little control over. If this was the case, what was he being paid for?

Why was a man who had little knowledge of the owners of his club, those who paid his wages and his bonuses, being consulted on footballing and monetary issues if he wasn't willing to put his foot down? Storrie knew of course that one wrong word to a family who had a history of arms dealing would mean the end of his job and the bonuses for nothing would instantly cease. Storrie even claimed he had received an offer to join another Premier league club for "a lot more money" yet he turned them down, in order to continue his work to "save" Pompey.

By March 2010, however, his position was finally seen as untenable – as it should have been for some time in truth – and he stepped down to allow Andronikou to deal with the administration, having previously assisted him. Despite leaving the club, to the fury of Pompey fans Storrie is still paid by Portsmouth, and still worked to "prepare" the club for it's FA Cup semi-final appearance against Tottenham Hotspur, now managed by none other than Harry Redknapp. Storrie is also a continuing influence as to who may take over the club, insisting he had a South African consortium who might purchase Portsmouth – which seemed to be apt timing as it would have coincided with the 2010 World Cup in South Africa. According to the *Daily Mirror*, Storrie was still so attached to the club that he was having his suit and shoes made by the same stylists as then manager Avram Grant and the Pompey players for their pre-match stroll at the Cup final.

Of course ultimately there is no one person to blame for Portsmouth's plight, but there are far fewer than one may initially expect. In short, each owner bares the responsibility, but any person in a position of power at the club, whether it be Storrie or Sacha Gaydamak, has had ample time, and funding, in order to revitalise and rescue Portsmouth.

The Gaydamak fiasco is possibly the biggest reason, at least, in recent memory, that the club find themselves in their present position. Despite allegedly asset stripping the club, Gaydamak is still a major creditor and is claiming £30m owed to him. He has met with the administrators regarding his claim as well as discussing the ownership of land around the stadium. Gaydamak himself owns around ten acres to the west and north of Fratton Park and it has often been discussed amongst Portsmouth fans that the most likely scenario regarding the ground would be that it could be demolished to make way for a completely different business, most likely a supermarket.

As an article in the *Daily Mail* revealed, regarding Gaydamak's land ownership, "it is who owns the real estate – and what they do with it – that looks certain to determine the 112-year-old club's destiny. And if the club ceased to exist, a sale of Fratton Park and the surrounding land would become a far simpler deal."

Colin Farmery, spokesman for the recently formed Portsmouth Supporters' Trust, was quoted in the same article as suggesting:

> "This is to do with property. But is it about people making short-term profit out of a property deal or making a long-term profit by using a property deal to develop the football club and turn it into a business which can be sold on five or 10 years down the line? The way the current owners have behaved suggests their motivation is more short-term than long-term."

It is certainly not a giant leap to presume the ownership of Portsmouth has recently hinged upon who would be most accomplished to develop the land under which Fratton Park stands, given their recent owners all have ties with real estate in one form or another. Is it a stretch to suggest that the club are being purposely run into the ground in order to quickly and easily demolish Fratton Park and sell the land for major redevelopment? That is, after all, what property developers do. And if there were any care put into the development of Portsmouth FC rather than the land upon which they stand, which must be worth a whole lot more, then they would be in receipt of their own ground improvements and sensible investment as opposed to the melee they have recently been subjected to.

Gaydamak has since remained elusive and ignored all pleas to come forward and explain to the fans his role in the club's financial downfall. Even Uefa president Michel Platini has had a say in the "farce" at Pompey, claiming it "should have been prevented".

In a rare moment of insight and clarity, the former French midfield legend said, "I'm not an expert of finance, but it was easy to understand that clubs like Portsmouth would be in big danger of going bankrupt and going down. We have to protect them. Why was this club winning the FA Cup with losses of £50 million?" Though he makes a salient point, this is perhaps the misguided thinking we can all be guilty of within football circles. Modern thinking provides the opinion that in "winning" something, there must be financial reward. That in winning the FA Cup as a Premier League team, there must be level headed thinking in the boardroom. Of course, there is a financial reward for winning a trophy, just as there is for finishing 15th in the Premier league. But the reward is meaningless if a club is £120m in debt. Equally, should the joy and glory of winning a cutthroat competition such as the FA Cup be tempered by the assertion that the club must be worth something extra because of it?

Anyone can win the Cup, and in an ironic twist of modern football, they are probably more likely to. With the big clubs resting their main players for the trophies which are considered less important, there is far more of a level playing field for the remaining contestants. That is how Ross County can reach a Scottish Cup Final, and how Portsmouth, despite their financial record, can reach two in three years. It's not about money, playing well in a cup competition is about good management and hungry players.

This is why it is all the more doleful that Platini and Uefa agreed that Portsmouth were not allowed to enter Europe for the 2010/11 season, despite them once again defying the odds and reaching the final in 2010, where they met Chelsea. Ordinarily, with Chelsea a shoe-in for the Champions League, regardless of the outcome in the Cup Final Portsmouth would have reached the profitable hallowed ground known as the Europa League. Yet, in their infinite wisdom, the FA and the Premier league jointly decided that this should not be allowed, and even if it were approved by the domestic killjoys, Uefa would have not accepted a club who were in administration appearing in Europe.

Instead, Portsmouth fans had to suffer the greater indignity of the Premier League's seventh placed club receiving a spot in the Europa league instead. No matter how badly run a football club may be, the ultimate prize for British clubs – a place in European competition – should surely not be jeopardised by the quite farcical organising behind the Champions League (which features third and fourth placed sides from leagues in a competition where they are supposed to be the best teams in their respective country) and the increasingly bizarre and ever changeable Uefa Cup, now known as the Europa League, in which any team who once played in Iceland during the 1960s can qualify and play other teams in a mish-mash of matches that are ever more confusing until we finally see a final between two teams who could have just played the one match and saved us all a lot of bother.

Regardless, the excitement of your club reaching European competition, the travelling and the new experiences and match-ups are to be savoured by any team who perform well enough in the preceding season, and it's being denied the players and fans of Portsmouth for no fault of their own. Andrew Andronikou agreed, saying, "It's wrong for the fans that they should not be allowed to support their club in Europe next season. Last week they were asking us to prepare an application and now they are saying they won't consider one."

Despite this monetary melee, despite certain players not being eligible to appear for the club, despite the lack of funds to buy new players or at times pay their existing squad members, those in the trenches at the club have performed miracles to reach their second final in three years. Many of the stories here have been frightening at times and upsetting to those who love the game. In truth, a lot of the outcomes have been negative; how can one find a silver lining when a club cannot even sustain itself and play in the division in which it undoubtedly belongs? The financial problems of Leeds United spring to mind, and there is not even space to examine Charlton Athletic, Norwich City or Southampton.

With Portsmouth, who have undoubtedly had the roughest ride of the current high profile clubs, there indeed is a reason to be cheerful. Many of their players are British, as they are generally much cheaper, and this may in fact be the future. Whether or not it is down to their geographical and traditional make-up or not, the fact remains that the Portsmouth players who are still with the club are there for the love of the game, not to mention the club, and not financial gain. The players who once offered to accept a drop in wages – Michael Brown, Hermann Hreidarsson and David James – are all still with the club. Despite the ridiculous scenes in the boardroom those players have been staples of a team which has performed the archetypal cup fairy tale which every football fan loves to witness. It is a dream too unlikely to truly believe in but incredibly, Portsmouth somehow reached the Cup final at Wembley.

It brings to mind the belief that the game is stronger than any behind the scenes wranglings or even the greatest of farce. As the then Pompey manager Avram Grant commented, "Football should be decided on the pitch not in the courts, not in the Premier League offices." Football has always been a simple game and, regardless of the simple being made complex by the biggest airheads and crooked bodies to ever be involved in the game, it will most likely remain the same as it was in 1910: a green pitch with white markings with a goal at either end. Two teams of 11, battling to be victorious. When broken down to its core, football can and always will flourish. Those willing to forget the money makers and their dodgy dealings, those willing to sacrifice monetary reward for the love of the game, they are the glue which still holds the game together. As long as even just a fraction of the players believe in footballing – and not financial – glory, the game can remain beautiful.

Sources: *The Independent, The Times, The Sun, News Of The World, Guardian, Daily Mirror, Daily Telegraph, The First Post, Financial Times, The News, Daily Mail, Sky Sports, BBC, ITV, Fit And Proper Persons BBC South Documentary, Tony Husband.*

EPILOGUE

"I know what is around the corner – I just don't know where the corner is." – Kevin Keegan

At its heart football is a simple game. There are two teams of 11 both trying to score more goals than the other on a fairly basic set of lines painted onto grass. The best managers, certainly the most revered, are those who have taken this simplicity principle to its highest peak and filled their team talks with inspiring advice and rousing vitality. These managers avoid overanalysing and instead focus on steering their players into the right frame of mind. When football is overcomplicated, it becomes less fun. As Brian Clough once said, "Players lose you games, not tactics. There's so much crap talked about tactics by people who barely know how to win at dominoes."

By the same token, running a football club should also be simple. Perhaps not easy, but certainly simple. A squad of players, a manager, staff behind the scenes and an owner and/or chairman. Aside from the fans this should really be the staple of a football club. If we view the diagram below, we can see how football is presently constructed and also where it is currently going wrong.

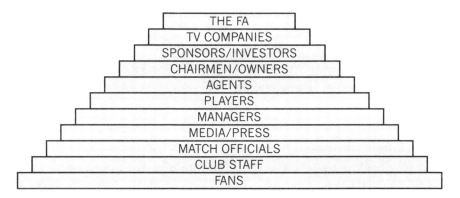

THE FA
TV COMPANIES
SPONSORS/INVESTORS
CHAIRMEN/OWNERS
AGENTS
PLAYERS
MANAGERS
MEDIA/PRESS
MATCH OFFICIALS
CLUB STAFF
FANS

It is clear, if we reverted to the original basics of the game where there were those who truly mattered running the club and getting involved, the problems behind the scenes would be smaller and more manageable. As you might suspect, this diagram shows who the real obstructions to this simplicity are.

To an extent the media and press are necessary, in order to keep clubs in the public eye and stir the interest enough for us to keep watching in the stands and paying the TV money for almost daily matches.

Having seen the melee behind the scenes at many football clubs, it is clear that the problems often occur behind the scenes in areas that don't really relate to football. Trade companies and individuals who have no relevance to the club become involved, chairmen and owners become keen on outside business which may increase a club's profits but actually has no relation to events on the pitch. Clubs become drowned in a sea of boardroom activities and external events which have nothing to do with football. Sponsors and investors to a palpable extent have ruined the basic ethics of running a football club.

The more sponsors and investors, the more complicated the finances, the more credit given, the more problems likely to be encountered down the road. The general public are regularly being told as a whole, and as individuals, that they need to reduce their debts and wherever possible consolidate them into one monthly payment. This is of course usually under a stack of additional, unnecessary interest which effectively means it will take you three times as long to pay what you already owed.

In the same way that we as individuals need to take the power back and dispense with credit cards, mortgages and loans, so too do the football clubs who are living a champagne lifestyle with a Lambrini budget. Eventually, as happens with people who become threatened with the apparent indignity of bankruptcy, football clubs fall into administration, which essentially means "you are not capable of handling your finances". Ironically, it is this opportunity – rather than a punishment – which can give new life and a clean slate.

Most high profile clubs were not in debt until the swarm of television greed engulfed them. With every match televised, even if in highlight form, the clubs become more scrutinised. Every transfer move is analysed, every step on the pitch computerised and spat out in a format which tells you your number six did quite a bit of leg work but couldn't pass the ball if his life depended on it.

As for agents, it's hard to find a reason that they exist, other than to bleed the clubs dry and make even more money for even more people who don't truly relate to the business of football. If you take out the agents, the superfluous trade companies, the investors who now want their money back, and the TV money, Portsmouth would not have needed to go into liquidation, and that's even with the group of cowboys who have overseen their finances for the last few years. Equally, if there were no agents the chances are the players would not have received such lavish, gratuitous contractual guarantees and wages.

So what is the alternative? Ultimately, as we can see from the power structure pyramid, the true power resides with the Premier League and the Football Association itself. It is not enough to send a belated loan to a club who are clearly about to drop into administration regardless (a la Portsmouth). It's like treating a sore throat with a lozenge instead of adopting the healthy lifestyle which would prevent you developing a sore throat in the first place: glossing over the symptoms instead of removing the cause in the beginning. The Premier League is supposedly the richest league in the world but this obviously does not take into account debts, simply the amount of money being generated. Beyond the owners themselves, the players, the TV companies and the sponsors, there is little actually being generated for the clubs themselves. Aside from the largest clubs, the majority of the league's teams are scrapping for survival on a daily basis, struggling to finish higher in the league yet finding the funding to purchase good enough players in order to do this an impossible task.

To some extent there has to be some design to this madness. In the same way that virtually every football fan can agree that goal-line technology should be used while Uefa continues to blatantly ignore the obvious improvements, there are many discrepancies that we can all see that are continually overlooked. The men who run football do not appear to be of lesser intelligence than your average primate, so why should they run a national institution with such flagrant disregard for what is right, not to mention common sense.

We are often told that the reason football cannot receive any rule changes or outside help to determine a just outcome is because the powers that be do not want to mess with the tradition of the game. Yet at the same time our game has been ripped to pieces by outside influences in the form of foreign investors who have no inkling about the game, finance companies, corporations, superfluous officials with no power to do anything, and, worst of all, flashing advertising boards that disrupt our enjoyment of the game. And yet Uefa don't want to hold up the game for one minute when trying to decipher if the ball really did cross the line or not.

In America's NFL, coaches of each team have "challenges" which can be used twice per half at any time after each play has been completed or an official's decision made. They throw a red flag to the ground to signal they wish to challenge the call that has been made. The officials then view the incident again and again until they reach a conclusion as to the right decision, which often only takes a few minutes. If the coach is correct the decision is overturned, if they are wrong they lose one of three time-outs they have per half. Pretty simple, and it works.

Football could certainly learn an awful lot from the NFL in matters relating to the game itself, but it is also the financial area in which the NFL surpasses British football in terms of common sense. One way in which the Premier League, or indeed any league in Britain, could improve is to change the way in which transfers are conducted. I would suggest agents are instantly outlawed; they serve no purpose that a non-profit Players Association or union could not manage. For the player, the only purpose of an agent is to make sure they are not ripped off and in the case of modern greed, to ensure a large one-off payment and a fat regular pay packet come what may.

For the clubs, the agent is an unwelcome distraction at best and a snakelike drain on resources at worst. The word kickback has no place in football other than to refer to a back heel. No one should receive a kickback from a deal between a club and a player; it is simply unethical and unnecessary. Therefore, if the Football Association were to govern the game properly they could create a system whereby every transfer fee was agreed between the two clubs with oversight from the FA. Once this is agreed, the club and player negotiate a deal – once again with oversight from the FA.

If the player is unhappy with the terms they would simply renegotiate until the terms were acceptable; if the terms were unacceptable, they would be open to offers again. When a deal is confirmed, the FA should then take a percentage of the fee which is then distributed back into the league. There should also be a portion of each fee which is distributed amongst the clubs in a manner which follows the NFL hierarchy. Each year the team with the worst record in the league will be granted the choice of the best young players coming through college. So effectively, for the 2009/2010 season if Manchester United had paid Lille £2 million for a player, £50,000 of that could have been given to Portsmouth, £40,000 to Burnley and so on...

Club's accounts could be scrutinised by the league on a regular basis – say, every six months – to ensure they are trading within their means and also running the club to the benefit of the club and its supporters. Providing they are being run efficiently then each club would be entitled to these bonuses, as it would be one way of ensuring they would *want* to remain solvent.

Clubs are punished by running their finances with abandon, should they not therefore receive the incentive of a reward should they run their finances competently?

Equally, a salary cap should be enforced with immediate effect. In the NFL, there is a minimum the club should be paying its players as well as a maximum – thus ensuring players are not ripped off but neither is the club. If these rules were applied across Uefa with immediate effect then the players would have no option but to play as much for the love of the game as the wages that would come with it. We are not talking a drop of £50,000 per week, but perhaps £25,000. Either way, it would be up to the clubs. If Didier Drogba wanted £200,000 a week but Chelsea's total cap was £500,000 it would be up to the owner's discretion as to whether this truly represented value for money and whether the remaining thirty players would want to spread the paltry £300,000 between them every week.

Quite simply the only way to run a football club in a solvent manner today is to dispense with the needless aspects behind the scenes and return the game to its rightful place where fans pay to see the team and the ticket sales pay players' wages. If the team are not performing then chances are the attendances are going to decrease. But the way to increase turnover is not to enter into sub-businesses and business which is outside of football. A football club should not be run by anyone other than a person who is knowledgeable about the sport.

The game is broken on so many levels and yet the same faces are always there propping the game up on its knees, seemingly oblivious to the problems the clubs which hold the game together are inevitably going to face. We see the same teams doing well every year, the same journeyman managers being bandied around from one crap team to the next; we are told these men are masters at avoiding the drop or stabilising a team but it seems to be more a case of them stabilising mediocrity so that the higher echelons remain where they belong. As we have seen, it is not just a case of money. Manchester United, Chelsea and Liverpool are not at the top because they are richer than other clubs. Nowadays any club can be bought by a billionaire; it means nothing because most of them have no idea how to run a football club.

So how is it the likes of Manchester United and Liverpool can change owners and yet remain at the top of the game? As we have examined, the same is also true in the Scottish game, with Celtic and Rangers the ever dominant force. In Italy, the top teams have always been AC Milan, Juventus and Internazionale and these teams are usually around the top of the league year upon year still. It is the same in Spain (Real Madrid, Barcelona) and indeed most other European countries. Why is this the case? The reasons are clearly complex, but once again the beautiful game should look to the NFL for an example of how to run a league.

The NFL consists of 32 teams and many of them have won the ultimate accolade in the game – the Superbowl. Though the best teams in the league qualify for play-offs each year, the play-offs up to and including the Superbowl are merely one-off games, which admittedly does have a slight effect on how capable a team are of winning the trophy.

Yet, the league is notoriously difficult to predict, with many teams easily able to bounce back following a losing season. Some can finish a season having lost 10 of 12 games or worse and then the following season return with an even record, or better. The reason for this is largely because of the fairness with which the NFL operates in spreading its considerable wealth among the various teams and allowing the weakest team each year to strengthen in key positions and mount a challenge. This way the league always remains competitive. There is simply no argument that this would not better the British game and it would mean that those teams who are always the nearly-men – managed by "been, there done it but not very well" managers – might just stand a chance of climbing the league.

For football to improve it needs to travel back in time and take the best of the modern improvements with it, of which it has to be said there aren't that many. So keep your modern footwear which is welded to the shape of a player's foot, but ditch the £9m in agents' fees for the month. Keep your ludicrous range of merchandise going because it benefits the club and we all love a crest covered rubber duck, but lose the £200 grand-a-week players. As we've seen they are probably not going to create you more profit – only debt. And that would truly be a waste of money.